# The Huge Book of Fascinating Facts

by
Jake Jacobs

* * * * *

Published by Jake Jacobs

The Huge Book of Fascinating Facts

# 1.

Benjamin Harrison was the 23rd President of the United States, serving from 1889 to 1893.

# 2.

He was born on August 20, 1833, in North Bend, Ohio.

# 3.

Harrison was the grandson of William Henry Harrison, the 9th President of the United States.

# 4.

He was the second President to have his grandfather also serve as President.

# 5.

Harrison graduated from Miami University in Oxford, Ohio, in 1852, and then studied law in Cincinnati.

# 6.

He enlisted as a private in the Union Army during the American Civil War and eventually rose to the rank of brigadier general.

# 7.

Harrison was known for his strong support for the Civil Rights Act of 1875, which aimed to protect the civil rights of African Americans.

# 8.

He served as a U.S. Senator from Indiana from 1881 to 1887.

# 9.

Harrison was a Republican and held conservative views on economic matters.

## 10.

He won the presidential election of 1888, defeating incumbent President Grover Cleveland.

## 11.

Harrison's presidency was marked by efforts to increase protective tariffs and support for industrialization.

## 12.

He signed the McKinley Tariff Act of 1890, which raised tariffs on imported goods.

## 13.

Harrison advocated for the conservation of natural resources and signed legislation establishing several national parks and forest reserves.

## 14.

He was the first President to install electricity in the White House.

## 15.

Harrison's administration saw the passage of the Sherman Antitrust Act, which aimed to regulate monopolistic business practices.

## 16.

He was an advocate for expanding American influence overseas and pursued an aggressive foreign policy.

## 17.

Harrison signed the Land Revision Act of 1891, which allowed for the sale of public lands in the western United States.

# 18.

During his presidency, the Pledge of Allegiance was first recited in schools.

# 19.

Harrison's administration negotiated several treaties, including the Bering Sea arbitration with Great Britain.

# 20.

He was known for his support of civil service reform and signed the Pendleton Civil Service Reform Act into law.

# 21.

Harrison was the first President to have his voice recorded.

# 22.

He lost his bid for re-election in 1892 to Grover Cleveland.

# 23.

After leaving the presidency, Harrison returned to practicing law in Indianapolis.

# 24.

He served as the counsel for Venezuela in the boundary dispute with Great Britain known as the Venezuela Crisis.

# 25.

Harrison was a founding member of the Society of the Cincinnati, an organization of Revolutionary War officers.

# 26.

He was known for his oratory skills and delivered many speeches throughout his political career.

# 27.

Harrison was a Freemason and served as Grand Master of the Grand Lodge of Indiana.

# 28.

He was an advocate for women's suffrage and supported the movement for women's rights.

# 29.

Harrison's wife, Caroline Harrison, was active in the Women's Christian Temperance Union and championed causes such as women's education and health.

# 30.

Harrison had two children, Russell and Mary, and both followed in his footsteps as lawyers.

# 31.

He was the last President to have a beard while in office.

# 32.

Harrison was an avid reader and collector of books.

# 33.

He was a lover of nature and enjoyed spending time outdoors, particularly at his home in Indianapolis.

# 34.

Harrison was a strong advocate for the construction of the Panama Canal.

# 35.

He was known for his strict work ethic and dedication to his duties
as President.

# 36.

Harrison was the first President to have his photograph taken while
in office.

# 37.

He was a skilled debater and often participated in public debates
during his political career.

# 38.

Harrison was known for his integrity and honesty.

# 39.

He was a supporter of the gold standard and opposed the free
coinage of silver.

# 40.

Harrison was a member of the Presbyterian Church and regularly
attended services.

# 41.

He was the first President to have his inaugural address recorded on
a phonograph.

# 42.

Harrison's presidency saw a significant expansion of the Navy, with
the construction of new battleships and cruisers.

# 43.

He appointed several African Americans to prominent government
positions, breaking racial barriers.

# 44.

Harrison was the first President to use the White House as the official name of the presidential residence.

# 45.

He served as the Commander-in-Chief of the Grand Army of the Republic, an organization of Union veterans.

# 46.

Harrison's administration advocated for the protection of American industries and supported high tariffs.

# 47.

He delivered his inaugural address on a bitterly cold day, without wearing a coat or hat, to demonstrate his toughness.

# 48.

Harrison's campaign slogan during the presidential election was "The People's Choice."

# 49.

He had a strong interest in Native American affairs and advocated for their rights.

# 50.

Harrison passed away on March 13, 1901, in Indianapolis, Indiana, at the age of 67.

# 51.

The Ipiutak site is an archaeological site located near Point Hope, Alaska, on the northwest coast of the state.

# 52.

It is named after the Ipiutak culture, which thrived in the region from approximately 200 BCE to 800 CE.

# 53.

The Ipiutak site is known for its well-preserved and elaborate ceremonial structures and burial sites.

# 54.

The site was first discovered in 1939 by archaeologist Froelich Rainey during an expedition led by the University Museum of the University of Pennsylvania.

# 55.

Excavations at the site have revealed a wealth of artifacts, including ivory and bone carvings, masks, figurines, and tools.

# 56.

The Ipiutak people were skilled hunters and gatherers, relying on marine resources such as seals, walruses, and fish.

# 57.

The site is believed to have been a major ceremonial center for the Ipiutak culture, with evidence of large communal buildings and structures.

# 58.

The architecture at the Ipiutak site is characterized by circular or oval-shaped structures made of driftwood, whalebone, and sod.

# 59.

The structures at the site were often decorated with elaborate carvings and painted designs.

# 60.

Excavations have uncovered numerous burials at the Ipiutak site, including both individual and mass graves.

# 61.

The burial sites contain a variety of grave goods, such as pottery vessels, hunting tools, and personal ornaments.

# 62.

The Ipiutak people practiced a form of artificial cranial deformation, in which the skulls of infants were bound to produce an elongated shape.

# 63.

The purpose of cranial deformation in Ipiutak society is still not fully understood, but it may have been a form of social distinction or an aesthetic preference.

# 64.

The Ipiutak site provides important insights into the religious and ceremonial practices of the ancient Arctic cultures.

# 65.

The site has been designated a National Historic Landmark, recognizing its significance in American history.

# 66.

The Ipiutak culture is believed to have had connections with other Arctic cultures, including the Thule and the ancient Yup'ik.

# 67.

The Ipiutak site is located on a high bluff overlooking the Chukchi Sea, offering stunning views of the surrounding landscape.

# 68.

Excavations at the site have revealed evidence of long-distance trade, with artifacts from as far away as Siberia and the Aleutian Islands.

# 69.

The Ipiutak people were skilled artisans, producing intricate carvings and sculptures from materials such as walrus ivory and whalebone.

# 70.

The site has provided valuable information about the effects of climate change on Arctic cultures, including shifts in subsistence strategies and settlement patterns.

# 71.

The Ipiutak site is considered one of the most important archaeological sites in Alaska.

# 72.

The artifacts found at the site have contributed significantly to our understanding of ancient Arctic cultures and their artistic traditions.

# 73.

The Ipiutak culture is believed to have declined around 800 CE, possibly due to a combination of environmental changes and social factors.

# 74.

The site has been the subject of ongoing research and excavations, with new discoveries and insights continuing to emerge.

# 75.

The Ipiutak site is a testament to the ingenuity and adaptability of ancient Arctic peoples in the face of challenging environmental conditions.

# 76.

The site provides evidence of long-term human occupation in the region, spanning several centuries.

# 77.

The Ipiutak people had a complex social organization, with evidence of hierarchical structures and specialized roles.

# 78.

The site's location near the coast suggests that the Ipiutak people relied heavily on marine resources for their survival.

# 79.

The Ipiutak site offers a glimpse into the spiritual beliefs and practices of the ancient Arctic cultures, with evidence of ritual activities and ceremonies.

# 80.

The site has yielded a large number of animal bones, providing valuable information about the ancient Arctic ecosystem and the hunting practices of the Ipiutak people.

# 81.

Excavations at the site have revealed evidence of house structures, indicating that the Ipiutak people lived in semi-subterranean dwellings.

# 82.

The Ipiutak site is characterized by its unique architectural style, with circular or oval-shaped structures that differ from the rectangular houses found in other Arctic cultures.

# 83.

The Ipiutak people had a sophisticated understanding of their environment, utilizing local resources and adapting to changing conditions.

## 84.

The site has been instrumental in shaping our understanding of the cultural and technological development of ancient Arctic societies.

## 85.

The Ipiutak culture is considered part of the broader Arctic Small Tool tradition, which encompasses a range of ancient cultures in the Arctic region.

## 86.

The Ipiutak site has been used as a point of reference for studying other ancient Arctic cultures and their connections.

## 87.

The site's preservation is a testament to the harsh Arctic climate, which has helped protect the artifacts and structures from decay.

## 88.

The Ipiutak people had a diverse diet, including marine mammals, fish, birds, and land mammals.

## 89.

The site has provided evidence of early human migration and settlement in the Arctic, shedding light on the peopling of the Americas.

## 90.

The Ipiutak culture is believed to have had a complex relationship with the environment, balancing resource extraction with sustainability.

# 91.

The Ipiutak site has been a source of inspiration for contemporary Arctic artists, who draw upon the rich cultural heritage of the region.

# 92.

The site has been a focus of cultural revitalization efforts, with local communities working to preserve and promote their ancestral heritage.

# 93.

The Ipiutak site offers a glimpse into the daily lives of the ancient Arctic peoples, revealing aspects of their technology, economy, and social organization.

# 94.

Excavations at the site have revealed evidence of seasonal occupation, suggesting that the Ipiutak people may have engaged in migratory patterns.

# 95.

The Ipiutak site has contributed to our understanding of ancient trade networks and the exchange of goods across vast distances.

# 96.

The site has been a site of pilgrimage and cultural significance for Indigenous communities in the region, who maintain a strong connection to their ancestral lands.

# 97.

The Ipiutak culture is recognized for its artistic achievements, with intricate carvings and sculptures that reflect their deep connection to the natural world.

# 98.

The site's archaeological importance extends beyond its local significance, providing valuable comparative data for studying ancient cultures around the world.

# 99.

The Ipiutak site has inspired scientific research and scholarly debates about the origins and development of Arctic cultures.

# 100.

The ongoing study of the Ipiutak site continues to deepen our understanding of the ancient Arctic world and its enduring legacy in the present day.

# 101.

African lions (Panthera leo) are the second-largest big cat species, after tigers.

# 102.

They are native to sub-Saharan Africa and can be found in savannahs, grasslands, and semi-arid regions.

# 103.

Lions are highly social animals and live in groups called prides, which typically consist of several related adult females, their offspring, and a coalition of males.

# 104.

The size of a pride can range from a few individuals to over 30 lions.

# 105.

Male lions have a distinctive mane, which varies in color and length depending on their age, genetics, and environmental factors.

# 106.

The mane serves as a form of protection during fights with other males and can also indicate their social status and attract mates.

# 107.

Female lions are responsible for the majority of the hunting within the pride, working together in coordinated efforts to bring down large prey.

# 108.

Lions are apex predators and primarily feed on large herbivores such as zebras, wildebeests, buffalos, and various antelope species.

# 109.

They have a powerful bite force, capable of crushing bones, which aids in their ability to kill and consume their prey.

# 110.

Lions are known for their distinctive roar, which can be heard from miles away and serves as a vocalization to communicate with other pride members.

# 111.

The roar of a lion is one of the loudest of any big cat species and can reach volumes of up to 114 decibels.

# 112.

Male lions have been observed roaring to assert their dominance and defend their territory from rival males.

# 113.

Lions are primarily nocturnal animals, with their activity peaking during the early morning and late evening hours.

# 114.

They have excellent night vision, which enables them to hunt
effectively in low-light conditions.

# 115.

Lions have a unique social structure where related females stay
together in the same pride for their entire lives, while males usually
leave the pride once they reach maturity.

# 116.

Male lions often form alliances called coalitions, which help them
increase their chances of taking over a pride and reproducing.

# 117.

The lifespan of a wild lion is typically around 10 to 14 years,
although some individuals have been known to live into their late
teens and early twenties.

# 118.

Lions are well-adapted to their environment, with sharp retractable
claws for gripping prey and rough tongues for cleaning bones.

# 119.

African lions have a specialized set of teeth designed for cutting
through flesh and shearing meat from bones.

# 120.

The gestation period for a lioness is approximately 110 days, and she
gives birth to a litter of one to four cubs.

# 121.

Lion cubs are born blind and helpless, and they rely on their mother
for nourishment and protection.

# 122.

It is common for lionesses within a pride to synchronize their breeding cycles, resulting in the simultaneous birth of multiple litters.

## 123.

The cubs stay with their mother for about two years, learning essential hunting and survival skills before becoming independent.

## 124.

African lions have a unique scent-marking behavior, where they use their urine, feces, and scratch marks to establish and defend their territory.

## 125.

The size of a lion's territory can vary depending on factors such as prey availability and competition with other prides or males.

## 126.

Male lions have been known to engage in intense territorial battles, sometimes resulting in injuries or even death.

## 127.

Lions have a well-developed sense of hearing and can detect the sounds of prey or potential threats from a considerable distance.

## 128.

Despite their size and strength, lions are capable of reaching speeds of up to 50 miles per hour (80 kilometers per hour) in short bursts.

## 129.

Lions have adapted to survive in various climates, ranging from the hot and arid regions of the Sahara Desert to the more tropical habitats of East Africa.

## 130.

The conservation status of African lions is classified as "Vulnerable" by the International Union for Conservation of Nature (IUCN), with their populations declining due to habitat loss, human-wildlife conflict, and poaching.

## 131.

Efforts are being made to conserve lion populations through protected areas, anti-poaching measures, and community-based conservation initiatives.

## 132.

The African lion is a symbol of strength, courage, and royalty in many cultures, often depicted in ancient art and heraldry.

## 133.

Lions play a crucial role in maintaining the balance of ecosystems by controlling herbivore populations and preventing overgrazing.

## 134.

Lions are highly intelligent animals and exhibit problem-solving skills and social behaviors, such as cooperation and reciprocity within their prides.

## 135.

They have a complex vocal repertoire, consisting of various roars, grunts, growls, and purrs, which serve different communication purposes.

## 136.

Lions have excellent camouflage with their tawny-colored fur, enabling them to blend into their surroundings and approach prey undetected.

# 137.

African lions have been featured prominently in popular culture, appearing in literature, movies, and even as national symbols for several countries.

# 138.

The Maasai people of East Africa have a long-standing relationship with lions, integrating them into their cultural traditions and folklore.

# 139.

Lions have been admired and revered by humans for thousands of years, with depictions of lions found in ancient Egyptian, Greek, and Roman art and mythology.

# 140.

African lions have a hierarchical social structure within prides, with dominant individuals having priority access to resources such as food and mating opportunities.

# 141.

Lions have well-developed muscles in their forelimbs, allowing them to deliver powerful swipes with their paws when hunting or defending themselves.

# 142.

The color of a lion's mane can indicate their age and overall health, with darker and fuller manes typically found on older, more dominant males.

# 143.

African lions have been known to form strong bonds with their pride members, engaging in social grooming and displays of affection.

# 144.

The roar of a lion can have a paralyzing effect on other animals, causing them to freeze in fear or flee from the area.

## 145.

Lions have a keen sense of smell, which they use to locate prey, mark their territory, and recognize other individuals within their pride.

## 146.

In some cultures, the lion has been associated with bravery and courage, making it a popular symbol in coats of arms, flags, and national emblems.

## 147.

African lions have been studied extensively by researchers, providing valuable insights into their behavior, ecology, and conservation needs.

## 148.

Lions have unique whisker spots above their upper lips, which can be used to identify individuals, similar to fingerprints in humans.

## 149.

The iconic lioness Maasai Mara in Kenya, known as "Elsa" from the book and film "Born Free," brought global attention to the conservation of African lions.

## 150.

African lions are charismatic and awe-inspiring creatures, capturing the imagination and admiration of people around the world with their beauty, strength, and majestic presence in the wild.

## 151.

John Hart (1711-1779) was an American farmer, politician, and Founding Father who played a significant role in the American Revolution.

## 152.

He was born on December 3, 1711, in Stonington, Connecticut, and later moved to Hopewell, New Jersey.

## 153.

Hart worked as a farmer and miller, cultivating his land and running a successful business.

## 154.

He became involved in local politics and served as a justice of the peace and a member of the New Jersey Provincial Assembly.

## 155.

Hart was elected to the Continental Congress in 1774 and continued to serve until 1777.

## 156.

He was known for his strong support of American independence and was one of the signers of the Declaration of Independence.

## 157.

Hart's signature on the Declaration of Independence is distinctive, with the "J" in John and the "H" in Hart written in a larger size.

## 158.

During the Revolutionary War, Hart's property was destroyed by British troops, forcing him and his family to go into hiding.

## 159.

He spent several months moving from place to place to avoid capture by the British, often living in forests and caves.

## 160.

Despite the hardships, Hart remained committed to the cause of American independence and continued to serve in the Continental Congress.

## 161.

After the war, Hart returned to his farm in Hopewell and worked to rebuild his life and community.

## 162.

He served as a member of the New Jersey Legislature and as the speaker of the assembly.

## 163.

Hart was known for his humility and modesty, choosing a simple and quiet life over wealth and fame.

## 164.

He was a devout Christian and believed in the importance of moral values and civic duty.

## 165.

Hart married Deborah Scudder in 1739, and they had 13 children together, although some sources suggest the number may have been higher.

## 166.

His wife, Deborah, passed away in 1776, just a few months before Hart signed the Declaration of Independence.

## 167.

Hart's family was deeply affected by the war, and two of his sons served in the Continental Army.

## 168.

Despite the challenges and sacrifices, Hart remained committed to the cause of liberty and the principles of the American Revolution.

## 169.

He was known for his strong principles and unwavering dedication to the ideals of freedom and self-governance.

## 170.

Hart was well-respected by his fellow delegates in the Continental Congress and was known for his sound judgment and wisdom.

## 171.

After his term in Congress ended, Hart retired from public life and focused on his family and farming.

## 172.

He died on May 11, 1779, at the age of 67, and was buried in the churchyard of the First Baptist Church in Hopewell.

## 173.

In his honor, the John Hart Memorial Park was established in Hopewell to commemorate his contributions to the American Revolution.

## 174.

Hart's legacy lives on as one of the courageous signers of the Declaration of Independence, who risked everything for the cause of liberty.

## 175.

He is remembered as a patriot and a champion of freedom, whose actions helped shape the course of American history.

## 176.

The story of Hart's escape and his dedication to the cause of independence has been immortalized in various books, documentaries, and historical accounts.

## 177.

Hart's descendants continue to honor his memory and his contributions to the nation's founding.

## 178.

Several places and institutions have been named in honor of John Hart, including schools, parks, and historical sites.

## 179.

In 1969, John Hart was depicted on a United States postage stamp as part of the "Signers of the Declaration of Independence" series.

## 180.

Hart's life and achievements are celebrated annually on Independence Day, as his role in securing America's freedom is recognized and honored.

## 181.

His story serves as a reminder of the sacrifices made by the Founding Fathers and the enduring principles upon which the United States was built.

## 182.

The John Hart House, located in Hopewell, New Jersey, is a historic site that has been preserved and open to the public.

# 183.

Hart's role as a signer of the Declaration of Independence has cemented his place in American history and the fight for independence.

# 184.

The act of signing the Declaration of Independence was a treasonous act against the British crown, demonstrating Hart's courage and commitment to the cause.

# 185.

Despite his public service, Hart remained a humble and down-to-earth individual, prioritizing the well-being of his family and community.

# 186.

The exact details of Hart's escape during the Revolutionary War remain somewhat shrouded in mystery, adding intrigue to his story.

# 187.

Hart's contribution to the founding of the United States extends beyond his role as a signer of the Declaration of Independence.

# 188.

He was a firm believer in the principles of individual liberty, limited government, and the pursuit of happiness.

# 189.

Hart's dedication to public service and his willingness to put his life and property at risk for the sake of liberty set an inspiring example for future generations.

# 190.

In 2011, the Hopewell Museum in New Jersey held a year-long exhibition to commemorate the 300th anniversary of John Hart's birth.

## 191.

Hart's commitment to the American Revolution and his refusal to waver in the face of adversity earned him the respect and admiration of his contemporaries.

## 192.

In 1889, a monument was erected in Hopewell to honor John Hart and his fellow New Jersey signers of the Declaration of Independence.

## 193.

Hart's experiences during the war and his dedication to the cause of independence highlight the sacrifices made by the Founding Fathers and their families.

## 194.

His role as a signer of the Declaration of Independence marked a significant step forward in the fight for American independence and the establishment of a new nation.

## 195.

Hart's story serves as a reminder of the hardships endured by those who fought for freedom and the principles upon which the United States was founded.

## 196.

The courage and conviction displayed by Hart and his fellow signers continue to inspire and influence American ideals and values.

## 197.

In 2020, a statue of John Hart was unveiled in New Jersey's capital city, Trenton, to honor his contributions to American history.

## 198.

Hart's commitment to liberty and self-governance exemplifies the spirit of the American Revolution and the founding principles of the United States.

## 199.

The legacy of John Hart is celebrated by historians, scholars, and Americans who recognize the significance of his contributions to the nation's founding.

## 200.

His name and story are forever etched in the annals of American history, serving as a reminder of the courage, determination, and sacrifice that paved the way for a free and independent nation.

## 201.

Kennecott Mines, also known as Kennecott Copper Mine, is located in Wrangell-St. Elias National Park and Preserve in Alaska, USA.

## 202.

The mine was named after Kennicott Glacier, but due to a clerical error, the spelling was changed to "Kennecott."

## 203.

Kennecott Mines operated from 1903 to 1938 and was one of the richest copper mines in the world.

## 204.

The mine was discovered by prospectors Jack Smith and Clarence Warner in 1900.

# 205.

It was founded by the Kennecott Copper Corporation, which was later acquired by the Kennecott Copper Company.

# 206.

The Kennecott Mines were responsible for producing over 4.6 million tons of copper ore during their operation.

# 207.

At its peak, the mine employed around 600 workers and had a population of over 300 people in the nearby town.

# 208.

The mine site included not only the copper mine but also a mill, power plant, railroad, and various support buildings.

# 209.

Kennecott Mines played a crucial role in the electrification of the United States, as it provided copper for wiring and electrical infrastructure.

# 210.

The mine was known for its innovative mining methods, including the use of steam shovels and rail transport for ore extraction.

# 211.

The Kennecott Mines are surrounded by stunning natural beauty, with rugged mountains, glaciers, and the Copper River flowing nearby.

# 212.

The area is home to diverse wildlife, including bears, moose, eagles, and salmon.

# 213.

The mine site is a National Historic Landmark and a popular tourist attraction, offering guided tours to visitors.

# 214.

The iconic red buildings at the mine site, including the Concentration Mill and the Power Plant, are a testament to its historical significance.

# 215.

The Kennecott Mines were featured in the National Geographic Channel's television series "Life Below Zero."

# 216.

The mine was abandoned in 1938 due to declining copper prices and the depletion of accessible ore.

# 217.

After its closure, the Kennecott Mines remained largely untouched for decades, preserving its industrial heritage.

# 218.

In 1986, the National Park Service acquired the Kennecott Mines and began efforts to preserve and stabilize the historic structures.

# 219.

Today, the mine site is managed as part of Wrangell-St. Elias National Park and Preserve, the largest national park in the United States.

# 220.

The Kennecott Mines attract thousands of visitors each year who come to explore the well-preserved buildings and learn about the mining history.

# 221.

The mine site offers guided tours that take visitors inside the mill, powerhouse, and other buildings, providing insights into the mining operations.

# 222.

The iconic 14-story Concentration Mill was once the tallest wooden building in North America.

# 223.

The mill was designed to process over 12,000 tons of ore per day, utilizing gravity separation and flotation techniques.

# 224.

The Powerhouse at Kennecott Mines housed several generators that produced electricity for the mine and the nearby town.

# 225.

The mine site is known for its engineering marvels, including the massive timber cribbing used to stabilize the structures on the steep hillside.

# 226.

The Kennecott Mines were a self-contained community, with housing, a hospital, a school, a store, and recreational facilities for the workers and their families.

# 227.

During its operation, the mine produced not only copper but also significant amounts of gold, silver, and other minerals.

# 228.

The ore extracted from the mine was transported by rail to Cordova, Alaska, and then shipped to smelters in Tacoma, Washington.

## 229.

The Kennecott Mines played a role in the economic development of Alaska and the growth of the railroad industry in the region.

## 230.

The area around Kennecott Mines offers numerous hiking and outdoor recreational opportunities, including exploring nearby glaciers and hiking trails.

## 231.

The rugged terrain and harsh climate posed significant challenges to the mining operations at Kennecott.

## 232.

The workers at the mine faced difficult working conditions, including extreme cold, avalanches, and the risk of cave-ins.

## 233.

The mine site has been used as a filming location for various movies and documentaries, including the film "The Hunt for Red October."

## 234.

The National Park Service conducts ongoing efforts to preserve and stabilize the historic structures at the mine site.

## 235.

In 1987, the Kennecott Mines were designated as a National Historic Landmark District for their architectural and historical significance.

## 236.

The mine site offers panoramic views of the surrounding mountains and glaciers, making it a popular spot for photography enthusiasts.

## 237.

The area around the Kennecott Mines is known for its rich geological history and is part of the Wrangell Volcanic Field.

## 238.

The mine site is a popular destination for outdoor enthusiasts, offering opportunities for camping, hiking, and wildlife viewing.

## 239.

The Kennecott Mines are a testament to the pioneering spirit of the early miners who braved the wilderness in search of riches.

## 240.

The historical significance of the Kennecott Mines lies not only in its mining operations but also in the social and economic impact it had on the region.

## 241.

The mine site provides valuable insights into the history of industrialization and mining practices in the early 20th century.

## 242.

The Kennecott Mines serve as a reminder of the boom and bust cycles that often characterize extractive industries.

## 243.

The preservation efforts at the mine site aim to maintain the historical integrity of the structures while ensuring visitor safety.

## 244.

The mine site offers educational programs and exhibits that explore the natural and cultural history of the area.

## 245.

The Kennecott Mines are a popular destination for photographers, who capture the unique combination of industrial ruins and natural beauty.

## 246.

The mine site is accessible by road, and visitors can reach it by driving the McCarthy Road, a gravel road that winds through the scenic wilderness.

## 247.

The Kennecott Mines attract researchers and historians interested in studying the mining history and the impact of mining on the environment and society.

## 248.

The area around the mine site is home to several species of wildlife, including Dall sheep, caribou, wolves, and migratory birds.

## 249.

The Kennecott Mines have been featured in several books, documentaries, and articles highlighting their historical and cultural significance.

## 250.

The preservation of the Kennecott Mines ensures that future generations can appreciate and learn from this important chapter in Alaska's history.

## 251.

African Penguins, also known as Black-footed Penguins or Jackass Penguins, are native to the coastal areas of southern Africa.

# 252.

They are the only penguin species that breeds in Africa.

# 253.

African Penguins are medium-sized penguins, standing about 60-70 cm (24-28 inches) tall and weighing around 2.2-3.5 kg (4.9-7.7 pounds).

# 254.

These penguins have a distinctive appearance with a black body and a white belly, along with black stripes and spots on their chest and face.

# 255.

African Penguins have a pink gland above their eyes that helps regulate their body temperature.

# 256.

They have short, stiff feathers that provide insulation and help keep them warm in cold water.

# 257.

African Penguins are well adapted for swimming and can reach speeds of up to 20 miles per hour (32 km/h) in the water.

# 258.

They have streamlined bodies and strong, flipper-like wings that enable them to be efficient swimmers.

# 259.

African Penguins are highly social birds and live in large colonies that can consist of thousands of individuals.

# 260.

They have a complex vocal repertoire and use various calls to communicate with each other.

# 261.

African Penguins are monogamous and form long-lasting pair bonds with their mates.

# 262.

They return to the same nesting site each year and typically lay two eggs in a burrow or nest made of guano (bird droppings) and debris.

# 263.

Both parents take turns incubating the eggs, which typically hatch after about 38-42 days.

# 264.

African Penguin chicks have fluffy gray plumage and gradually develop their adult feathers over several months.

# 265.

Parents regurgitate partially digested fish to feed their chicks.

# 266.

African Penguins primarily feed on small fish, such as anchovies and sardines, which they catch by swimming underwater using their wings as flippers.

# 267.

They have sharp, backward-pointing spines on their tongues and roofs of their mouths that help them grip and swallow slippery fish.

# 268.

African Penguins can dive to depths of around 130 meters (427 feet) in search of food.

## 269.

They have a gland located near their tail called the supraorbital gland, which filters salt from their bloodstream and helps them excrete excess salt through their nostrils.

## 270.

African Penguins are excellent swimmers but clumsy on land due to their short legs and webbed feet.

## 271.

They use a unique "foot-propelled" method to move on land, shuffling and sliding on their bellies or using their flippers to push themselves forward.

## 272.

African Penguins have a lifespan of about 10-15 years in the wild, although some individuals have been known to live into their 20s.

## 273.

They face several threats in the wild, including habitat loss, pollution, overfishing, and predation by seals and sharks.

## 274.

African Penguins are classified as an endangered species by the IUCN (International Union for Conservation of Nature).

## 275.

Conservation efforts are underway to protect African Penguin populations, including the establishment of protected areas and the rescue and rehabilitation of injured birds.

# 276.

Several colonies of African Penguins can be visited by tourists in South Africa and Namibia, providing opportunities for educational experiences and ecotourism.

# 277.

African Penguins are popular and charismatic animals, attracting the attention and interest of people worldwide.

# 278.

They are sometimes referred to as "jackass" penguins due to their distinctive braying call, which resembles the sound of a donkey.

# 279.

African Penguins have specialized feathers that help waterproof their bodies and provide insulation.

# 280.

The black and white coloration of African Penguins acts as camouflage, making them difficult to spot both from above and below the water.

# 281.

African Penguins have excellent eyesight, both in and out of the water, which helps them locate prey and avoid predators.

# 282.

African Penguins molt their feathers once a year, during which time they are unable to swim and must fast until their new feathers grow.

# 283.

The guano (bird droppings) produced by African Penguins is rich in nutrients and has been historically harvested for use as fertilizer.

# 284.

African Penguins have an acute sense of hearing, which helps them locate their mates and chicks within the noisy colony.

# 285.

They have a dense layer of fat called blubber, which helps insulate them in cold water.

# 286.

African Penguins have a high metabolic rate, allowing them to generate heat and maintain their body temperature in chilly ocean waters.

# 287.

They have a gland located above their eyes that secretes an oil-like substance, which they spread on their feathers to make them more waterproof.

# 288.

African Penguins engage in a behavior known as "porpoising," where they leap out of the water while swimming, resembling the movement of dolphins or porpoises.

# 289.

African Penguins have sharp beaks with backward-pointing spines, which help them catch and hold onto slippery prey.

# 290.

They have a specialized gland near their tail that produces a pungent odor, which they use for marking their territories and communicating with other penguins.

# 291.

African Penguins engage in mutual preening, where they groom each other's feathers using their beaks.

# 292.

They have an excellent sense of smell, which they use to locate their burrows or nests within the colony.

# 293.

African Penguins are agile and can navigate rocky coastal areas with ease, using their claws for grip.

# 294.

They are known to engage in courtship displays, including bowing, calling, and performing ritualized movements, to attract mates.

# 295.

African Penguins are vulnerable to oil spills, as their feathers lose their waterproofing ability when covered in oil, leading to hypothermia and death.

# 296.

They have a unique pattern of spots on their chests, which acts as an individual identifier and helps with recognition within the colony.

# 297.

African Penguins can hold their breath for several minutes while diving, allowing them to search for food underwater.

# 298.

They have a complex social hierarchy within the colony, with dominant individuals having preferential access to resources and breeding opportunities.

# 299.

African Penguins have specialized salt-excreting glands located above their eyes, which help them cope with the high salt content of their diet.

## 300.

African Penguins are a cherished species and have become an iconic symbol of African wildlife, captivating the hearts of people around the world.

## 301.

John Haviland was an American architect who lived from 1792 to 1852.

## 302.

He was born in Philadelphia, Pennsylvania, and spent most of his career working in the city.

## 303.

Haviland was known for his contributions to Greek Revival architecture in the United States.

## 304.

One of his most famous works is the Eastern State Penitentiary in Philadelphia, which is considered a masterpiece of Gothic architecture.

## 305.

Eastern State Penitentiary was the first prison of its kind in the United States and introduced the concept of solitary confinement.

## 306.

Haviland designed numerous public buildings, churches, and private residences throughout Philadelphia and the surrounding region.

# 307.

He also worked on projects in other states, including New Jersey, Maryland, and Virginia.

# 308.

Haviland's architectural style was characterized by clean lines, symmetry, and classical elements inspired by ancient Greek and Roman architecture.

# 309.

He was a proponent of the Philadelphia School of Architecture, which emphasized simplicity and restraint in design.

# 310.

Haviland's buildings often featured prominent porticos, columns, and pediments, which were common elements of Greek Revival architecture.

# 311.

He was known for his attention to detail and the use of high-quality materials in his constructions.

# 312.

Haviland's designs were influenced by his travels to Europe, where he studied classical architecture and observed architectural trends.

# 313.

He was a contemporary of other prominent architects of his time, including Benjamin Latrobe and William Strickland.

# 314.

Haviland's works helped shape the architectural landscape of Philadelphia and contributed to its reputation as a city of great architectural significance.

## 315.

In addition to his architectural career, Haviland was involved in civic and cultural activities in Philadelphia.

## 316.

He served as a director of the Pennsylvania Academy of the Fine Arts and was a member of various artistic and intellectual societies.

## 317.

Haviland was known for his dedication to the advancement of education and the arts.

## 318.

He was a strong advocate for the preservation of historical landmarks and played a role in the establishment of the Philadelphia Historical Commission.

## 319.

Haviland's architectural designs were often praised for their elegance, functionality, and adaptability to changing needs.

## 320.

His buildings were known for their durability and ability to withstand the test of time.

## 321.

Haviland's designs were not limited to grand public buildings but also included practical and utilitarian structures, such as warehouses and factories.

## 322.

He had a keen understanding of the relationship between architecture and the natural environment, and his designs often incorporated elements of nature.

## 323.

Haviland's works contributed to the growth and development of Philadelphia as an industrial and cultural hub in the 19th century.

## 324.

He was admired for his innovative use of materials and construction techniques, which allowed for the creation of large, open spaces in his buildings.

## 325.

Haviland's designs reflected the changing social and cultural climate of the time, as well as the aspirations of a growing nation.

## 326.

He was known for his ability to adapt his designs to different architectural styles, depending on the preferences of his clients.

## 327.

Haviland's architectural legacy extends beyond his own works, as he influenced and inspired future generations of architects.

## 328.

Many of his buildings have been recognized as historic landmarks and continue to be admired for their architectural significance.

## 329.

Haviland's designs were characterized by a sense of proportion, balance, and harmony, which created a pleasing visual effect.

## 330.

He was a versatile architect who was able to work on a wide range of
projects, from small-scale residential buildings to large-scale
institutional structures.

## 331.

Haviland's commitment to his craft and his attention to detail earned
him a reputation as one of the finest architects of his time.

## 332.

He believed that architecture should not only be functional but also
uplift the human spirit and contribute to the overall well-being of
society.

## 333.

Haviland's architectural philosophy emphasized the importance of
creating spaces that are conducive to human interaction and promote
a sense of community.

## 334.

He believed in the power of architecture to shape and influence
social behavior and was a strong advocate for the creation of well-
designed public spaces.

## 335.

Haviland's designs often incorporated natural light and ventilation,
creating comfortable and inviting environments.

## 336.

He was known for his ability to work within budget constraints
without compromising the quality of his designs.

## 337.

Haviland's designs were characterized by their timelessness, as they
continue to be appreciated and admired by architects and historians
today.

## 338.

He was a meticulous planner and took into consideration factors such as site orientation, climate, and functionality when designing his buildings.

## 339.

Haviland's buildings often featured innovative structural systems, allowing for large, open interior spaces free from the constraints of traditional load-bearing walls.

## 340.

He was known for his collaborative approach to design, often working closely with engineers and craftsmen to ensure the successful execution of his vision.

## 341.

Haviland's works were not limited to Philadelphia, as his designs can be found in other parts of the United States as well.

## 342.

His designs were influenced by the principles of the Greek and Roman architectural orders, as well as the classical ideals of balance and symmetry.

## 343.

Haviland's works celebrated the beauty of simplicity and emphasized the importance of proportion and scale in architectural design.

## 344.

He believed that architecture should be responsive to its surroundings and should enhance the natural environment rather than overpower it.

# 345.

Haviland's designs often incorporated decorative elements inspired by nature, such as floral motifs and ornate carvings.

# 346.

He was a strong advocate for the use of locally sourced materials, both for their aesthetic qualities and their sustainability.

# 347.

Haviland's designs were ahead of their time in terms of their functionality and adaptability to changing needs and technological advancements.

# 348.

He believed in the power of architecture to shape and improve the lives of individuals and communities.

# 349.

Haviland's designs continue to inspire architects today, who look to his works for lessons in timeless design and thoughtful integration with the built environment.

# 350.

His contributions to the field of architecture have left a lasting impact, not only in Philadelphia but also in the broader history of American architecture.

# 351.

Edward "Ned" Hector was an African-American soldier who fought during the American Revolutionary War.

# 352.

He was born around 1744 in Chester County, Pennsylvania, which was a hotbed of revolutionary activity.

## 353.

Hector was of African and Native American descent, reflecting the diverse makeup of the colonial population.

## 354.

He is best known for his heroic actions during the Battle of Brandywine on September 11, 1777.

## 355.

During the battle, Hector served as a teamster in the Continental Army, responsible for transporting supplies and ammunition.

## 356.

As the battle unfolded, Hector found himself near a cannon that was about to be abandoned by retreating soldiers.

## 357.

Despite being a civilian, Hector took charge of the cannon and successfully fired it, holding back the British forces.

## 358.

His actions bought valuable time for the Continental Army to regroup and make a strategic retreat.

## 359.

Hector's bravery and determination inspired those around him and earned him the respect of his fellow soldiers.

## 360.

He became a symbol of African-American patriotism and courage during the Revolutionary War.

## 361.

Hector's actions at the Battle of Brandywine were praised by General George Washington, who commended his bravery and personally thanked him for his service.

## 362.

After the Battle of Brandywine, Hector continued to serve in the Continental Army and participated in several other battles, including the Battle of Germantown and the Battle of Monmouth.

## 363.

Despite facing racial discrimination and inequality, Hector remained dedicated to the cause of American independence.

## 364.

He was one of many African-Americans who fought for the patriot cause during the Revolutionary War, seeking freedom and equality through their service.

## 365.

After the war, Hector returned to his civilian life in Pennsylvania and worked as a farmer.

## 366.

He married and had children, and his descendants continued his legacy of patriotism and service.

## 367.

Hector's heroic actions were largely overlooked and forgotten for many years, as the contributions of African-Americans in the Revolutionary War were often marginalized.

## 368.

However, in recent years, efforts have been made to recognize and honor Hector's bravery and the contributions of African-Americans in the fight for American independence.

## 369.

In 2005, a monument honoring Ned Hector was erected near the site of the Battle of Brandywine in Pennsylvania.

## 370.

The monument serves as a reminder of the important role played by African-Americans in the Revolutionary War.

## 371.

Hector's story has been featured in books, documentaries, and educational materials, helping to shed light on the often untold stories of African-American soldiers during the war.

## 372.

His bravery and determination continue to inspire people today, particularly those fighting for equality and justice.

## 373.

Hector's legacy is a testament to the power of individual actions in shaping history and the importance of recognizing the contributions of all who fought for American independence.

## 374.

His story highlights the complexity of the Revolutionary War era, where individuals from diverse backgrounds united in the fight for freedom.

## 375.

Hector's courage and resilience serve as a reminder that the struggle for liberty and equality is ongoing and requires the collective efforts of all people.

## 376.

In addition to his military service, Hector was known for his skills as a blacksmith, which were highly valued during the time.

## 377.

He was a skilled craftsman and his blacksmithing abilities were essential for the production and repair of weapons and equipment during the war.

## 378.

Hector's commitment to the cause of independence extended beyond his military service. He was known to have contributed financially to the American cause, even at personal cost.

## 379.

Hector's story illustrates the challenges faced by African-Americans during the Revolutionary War, including the limitations imposed on their roles and opportunities.

## 380.

Despite these challenges, Hector's actions demonstrated his determination to fight for liberty and his unwavering belief in the principles of the American Revolution.

## 381.

The bravery and heroism displayed by individuals like Ned Hector helped to challenge societal norms and lay the groundwork for the eventual abolition of slavery in the United States.

## 382.

Hector's story serves as a reminder that the fight for freedom and equality is not limited to a single moment in history but is an ongoing struggle.

## 383.

He symbolizes the countless African-Americans who played vital
roles in the Revolutionary War and whose contributions have often
been overlooked or forgotten.

# 384.

The recognition and celebration of Ned Hector's bravery serve as an
important step towards a more inclusive and accurate understanding
of the Revolutionary War.

# 385.

Hector's legacy inspires individuals to stand up for what they believe
in and to fight for justice and equality.

# 386.

His story reminds us that heroism comes in many forms and that
ordinary people can make extraordinary contributions to history.

# 387.

Ned Hector's name is immortalized in history as a symbol of
courage, resilience, and the pursuit of freedom.

# 388.

His story encourages individuals to explore the rich and diverse
history of the American Revolution and to recognize the
contributions of people from all walks of life.

# 389.

Hector's actions at the Battle of Brandywine demonstrate the
importance of seizing opportunities and stepping up in times of
crisis.

# 390.

His example challenges us to consider how we can make a positive
impact in our own lives and communities.

# 391.

Hector's legacy continues to inspire African-Americans and others to overcome adversity and strive for greatness.

# 392.

His story reminds us that the fight for freedom and equality is an ongoing struggle that requires vigilance and perseverance.

# 393.

Ned Hector's bravery and patriotism serve as a reminder that the American Revolution was not just a fight for independence from British rule but also a battle for the ideals of liberty and equality.

# 394.

His story invites us to reflect on the sacrifices made by individuals like him and to honor their memory by working towards a more inclusive and just society.

# 395.

Ned Hector's heroic actions exemplify the courage and determination displayed by countless individuals who fought for American independence.

# 396.

He represents the often-overlooked contributions of African-Americans to the founding of the United States.

# 397.

Hector's story challenges the traditional narrative of the American Revolution and highlights the complex and diverse nature of the struggle for independence.

# 398.

The recognition of Ned Hector's bravery serves as a reminder that history is not a monolithic narrative but a collection of diverse and interconnected stories.

## 399.

His story invites us to question and expand our understanding of the past, acknowledging the voices and experiences of those who have been marginalized.

## 400.

Ned Hector's legacy reminds us of the power of individual actions and the capacity of ordinary people to shape the course of history.

## 401.

The African Spurred Tortoise, also known as the Sulcata Tortoise, is one of the largest species of tortoises in the world.

## 402.

It is native to the Sahel region of sub-Saharan Africa, spanning countries such as Senegal, Mauritania, and Chad.

## 403.

These tortoises have a lifespan of up to 70 years in the wild, and some individuals have been known to live even longer in captivity.

## 404.

African Spurred Tortoises have a distinctive appearance with a large, dome-shaped carapace (shell) and thick, scaly legs.

## 405.

The carapace can reach lengths of up to 3 feet (91 cm) and weigh over 100 pounds (45 kg) in some individuals.

## 406.

The carapace is typically tan or yellowish-brown in color, helping the tortoise blend into its arid environment.

## 407.

They have long, sturdy limbs adapted for digging and walking on sandy terrain.

## 408.

African Spurred Tortoises are herbivores, feeding on a diet of grasses, plants, and cacti.

## 409.

They have a unique adaptation called the "spur," which is a horn-like projection on each thigh that they use for defense.

## 410.

When threatened, they can retract their heads and limbs into their shells for protection.

## 411.

African Spurred Tortoises are well adapted to survive in hot and dry environments, as they can tolerate high temperatures and conserve water.

## 412.

They have a keen sense of smell and can locate water sources and food from long distances.

## 413.

These tortoises are excellent burrowers and create deep burrows to escape extreme temperatures and predators.

## 414.

The burrows they create can be up to 10 feet (3 meters) long and help regulate their body temperature.

# 415.

African Spurred Tortoises are solitary animals and prefer to live alone, except during mating season.

# 416.

Mating usually occurs during the rainy season when food is plentiful.

# 417.

Females lay clutches of eggs, typically between 15 to 30 eggs, in a shallow nest dug in the sand.

# 418.

The eggs hatch after an incubation period of around 90 to 120 days.

# 419.

Hatchlings are small and vulnerable, measuring only a few inches in length.

# 420.

African Spurred Tortoises grow rapidly during their first few years of life and can reach sexual maturity at around 10 to 15 years of age.

# 421.

They are known for their loud vocalizations, producing various sounds like hisses, grunts, and huffs.

# 422.

These tortoises are highly adaptable and have been introduced to other parts of the world, including the United States, where they thrive in warm climates.

# 423.

In their native range, African Spurred Tortoises are considered a species of concern due to habitat loss, poaching, and the pet trade.

# 424.

They have a significant cultural and symbolic value in many African societies and are associated with longevity and wisdom.

# 425.

African Spurred Tortoises are popular pets, but they require proper care and a large enclosure to accommodate their size.

# 426.

They have specific temperature and humidity requirements, and owners must provide a suitable diet to ensure their well-being.

# 427.

African Spurred Tortoises have strong jaws and can bite if they feel threatened, so handling should be done with caution and respect.

# 428.

These tortoises have a unique adaptation that allows them to absorb moisture from dew and humidity in the air, reducing their dependence on water sources.

# 429.

They are excellent swimmers and can move gracefully in water, using their legs and long neck to propel themselves.

# 430.

African Spurred Tortoises have an impressive sense of touch, as their entire body, including the shell, is covered in nerve endings.

# 431.

Their shell is made of keratin, the same material as human fingernails, and continues to grow throughout their lifetime.

# 432.

The shell acts as protection from predators and provides structural support for the tortoise's body.

# 433.

African Spurred Tortoises are crepuscular, meaning they are most active during the early morning and late afternoon.

# 434.

They are known to bask in the sun to regulate their body temperature and absorb UV rays, which is essential for their health.

# 435.

These tortoises have a keen sense of spatial awareness and can navigate their environment with precision.

# 436.

African Spurred Tortoises have been known to use their strong front legs to push obstacles out of their way, including rocks and fallen branches.

# 437.

They have a slow metabolism and can survive for long periods without food or water.

# 438.

In extreme conditions, African Spurred Tortoises can enter a state of torpor, reducing their metabolic rate to conserve energy.

# 439.

They have a fascinating immune system that enables them to heal wounds and fight off infections.

## 440.

African Spurred Tortoises have a strong bond with their environment and can navigate back to their home range even after being moved long distances.

## 441.

They play an important ecological role by dispersing seeds in their droppings, contributing to plant regeneration.

## 442.

These tortoises are highly resilient and can adapt to a wide range of habitats, including grasslands, savannas, and semi-desert regions.

## 443.

African Spurred Tortoises have been observed using their front legs to dig shallow depressions in the soil, which they then use as dust baths to clean their shells.

## 444.

They have a unique mating behavior called "ramming," where the male forcefully strikes the female with his shell during courtship.

## 445.

African Spurred Tortoises have a low reproductive rate, with females typically laying eggs only once or twice a year.

## 446.

They have an incredible ability to store and conserve water, allowing them to survive in arid environments with limited access to drinking water.

# 447.

The presence of African Spurred Tortoises in an ecosystem can have a positive impact on vegetation, as they help control the growth of grasses and plants.

# 448.

These tortoises have been admired and represented in various forms of art and folklore, symbolizing endurance, wisdom, and longevity.

# 449.

They have been featured in literature, films, and documentaries, further raising awareness about their unique characteristics and conservation status.

# 450.

African Spurred Tortoises are a fascinating and iconic species, representing the beauty and diversity of Africa's wildlife and serving as a reminder of the importance of conservation efforts to protect their natural habitats.

# 451.

African Wild Dogs, also known as African painted dogs or Cape hunting dogs, are highly social animals that live in packs.

# 452.

They are native to sub-Saharan Africa and can be found in various habitats, including grasslands, savannas, and woodland areas.

# 453.

African Wild Dogs have a unique coat pattern with patches of black, yellow, and white fur, giving them a distinctive appearance.

# 454.

Each individual has a unique coat pattern, making it easier to identify and track them in the wild.

## 455.

They are the most specialized and efficient hunters among African carnivores, with a success rate of up to 80% in capturing prey.

## 456.

African Wild Dogs are cooperative hunters and work together as a pack to bring down larger prey such as antelopes.

## 457.

They have long legs and a lean body, which helps them cover large distances while hunting.

## 458.

African Wild Dogs have large round ears, which are excellent for picking up distant sounds and communicating within the pack.

## 459.

They have a strong social structure within the pack, led by an alpha male and alpha female.

## 460.

The alpha female is the primary breeder and leads the pack during hunts, while the alpha male defends the territory.

## 461.

African Wild Dogs have a complex vocal repertoire, including a unique high-pitched "hoo" call that they use to communicate with pack members.

## 462.

They are highly intelligent animals, capable of problem-solving and displaying a range of behaviors, including cooperation and communication.

## 463.

African Wild Dogs have a gestation period of around 70 days, after which the alpha female gives birth to a litter of 6 to 16 pups.

## 464.

The entire pack takes care of the young, with individuals taking turns to provide food and protection.

## 465.

African Wild Dog pups are born with a dark coat and gradually develop their distinctive coat pattern as they grow.

## 466.

The survival rate of African Wild Dog pups is relatively low, with only a small percentage reaching adulthood.

## 467.

African Wild Dogs have a strong sense of hierarchy within the pack, and dominant individuals receive priority during feeding.

## 468.

They have a complex social structure that involves regular bonding activities such as grooming and playful interactions.

## 469.

African Wild Dogs are highly efficient runners and can maintain a speed of up to 37 mph (60 km/h) over long distances.

## 470.

They have a unique hunting strategy, using a combination of stamina, teamwork, and strategic positioning to exhaust and capture their prey.

# 471.

African Wild Dogs have a relatively low population size and are considered an endangered species due to habitat loss and human-wildlife conflict.

# 472.

They are excellent swimmers and can cross rivers and streams in search of prey.

# 473.

African Wild Dogs have a specialized hunting technique called "swarming," where they surround their prey and take turns to chase and bring it down.

# 474.

They have a high metabolic rate and require large territories to find enough food to sustain their pack.

# 475.

African Wild Dogs have a unique reproductive strategy called "cooperative breeding," where only the alpha female and alpha male breed, and other pack members assist in raising the pups.

# 476.

They have a specialized digestive system that allows them to efficiently extract nutrients from their prey, including bones and other tough parts.

# 477.

African Wild Dogs are non-territorial and have overlapping home ranges with other packs in the area.

# 478.

They have a strong sense of smell and use scent markings to communicate with other packs and individuals.

# 479.

African Wild Dogs have a lifespan of around 10 to 12 years in the wild, but individuals in captivity can live longer.

# 480.

They are highly vulnerable to diseases such as rabies and distemper, which can have devastating effects on their populations.

# 481.

African Wild Dogs are known for their strong social bonds and exhibit a range of behaviors such as greeting ceremonies and vocalizations to strengthen group cohesion.

# 482.

They have excellent hearing and can detect the calls of their pack members from several miles away.

# 483.

African Wild Dogs have a unique hunting success rate compared to other large predators such as lions and hyenas.

# 484.

They have a specialized tooth structure, with large premolars for slicing through meat and sharp carnassial teeth for tearing.

# 485.

African Wild Dogs have a relatively high metabolic rate and need to consume large amounts of food to sustain their energy levels.

## 486.

They are known for their exceptional endurance and can cover long distances during a single hunting session.

## 487.

African Wild Dogs are important ecosystem engineers, as their hunting activities help control herbivore populations and shape vegetation dynamics.

## 488.

They have a keen sense of sight, allowing them to spot prey from a distance and coordinate their hunting strategies.

## 489.

African Wild Dogs have a matriarchal system within the pack, where the alpha female holds a dominant position and makes important decisions.

## 490.

They are highly nomadic and can travel several miles in search of prey or suitable denning sites.

## 491.

African Wild Dogs have a symbiotic relationship with certain bird species, such as the African pied crow, which follows them to scavenge on their kills.

## 492.

They are agile and can make quick turns while running, allowing them to navigate through dense vegetation during hunts.

## 493.

African Wild Dogs have a highly efficient cooling system, as they dissipate heat through their large, thin-walled ears.

# 494.

They have a unique social structure that allows for cooperative breeding, minimizing competition among pack members.

# 495.

African Wild Dogs are skilled at avoiding conflict within the pack and use various body language signals to communicate their intentions.

# 496.

They have a relatively high vocalization repertoire, including yelps, whines, and growls, which they use for communication and maintaining group cohesion.

# 497.

African Wild Dogs are known to show strong family bonds, with pack members caring for injured or sick individuals and providing support during challenging times.

# 498.

They are opportunistic feeders and will scavenge on the kills of other predators if the opportunity arises.

# 499.

African Wild Dogs have a keen sense of hearing, allowing them to detect prey or potential threats even in dense vegetation.

# 500.

They are charismatic and captivating animals, known for their unique coat pattern, cooperative hunting behavior, and important ecological role in African ecosystems.

# 501.

Patrick Henry was born on May 29, 1736, in Hanover County, Virginia.

# 502.

He was an American attorney, planter, and politician and is best known for his powerful oratory skills and speeches during the American Revolution.

# 503.

Henry was a staunch advocate for American independence and is famously remembered for his words, "Give me liberty, or give me death!"

# 504.

He served as the first and sixth Governor of Virginia, playing a crucial role in shaping the early years of the state and its independence.

# 505.

Henry was a member of the Virginia House of Burgesses, where he became a prominent voice against British colonial policies.

# 506.

He participated in the First Continental Congress in 1774, where he delivered his influential speech against the Stamp Act.

# 507.

Patrick Henry was a prominent supporter of the revolutionary cause and pushed for the formation of citizen militias to defend against British aggression.

# 508.

He was known for his passionate and persuasive speaking style, captivating audiences with his fiery rhetoric and impassioned pleas for liberty.

## 509.

Henry played a key role in the Virginia Convention of 1775, where he delivered his famous "Give me liberty, or give me death!" speech, urging Virginians to take up arms against British tyranny.

## 510.

He was a strong proponent of individual rights and personal freedoms, emphasizing the importance of limited government and the protection of civil liberties.

## 511.

Patrick Henry was a prominent Anti-Federalist, opposing the ratification of the United States Constitution due to concerns about centralization of power and the lack of a Bill of Rights.

## 512.

He eventually supported the Constitution after the promise of amendments, including the Bill of Rights, which he believed would safeguard individual liberties.

## 513.

Henry's speeches and writings, including his influential "Virginia Resolves," contributed to the growing sentiment of rebellion and helped galvanize public support for independence.

## 514.

He was a firm believer in the power of the people and their right to self-governance, advocating for democratic principles and participatory government.

## 515.

Patrick Henry was an influential figure in the creation of the Virginia Declaration of Rights, which later served as a model for the Bill of Rights in the United States Constitution.

# 516.

He was an early proponent of religious freedom, championing the separation of church and state and advocating for the disestablishment of the Anglican Church in Virginia.

# 517.

Henry's political career extended beyond his role as governor, as he also served in the Virginia House of Delegates and as a delegate to the Constitutional Convention in 1787.

# 518.

He opposed the centralization of power in the federal government and voiced concerns about the potential for tyranny if individual rights were not adequately protected.

# 519.

Henry was an influential figure in the formation of political parties in the United States, aligning himself with the Anti-Federalist faction and later becoming a leader of the Democratic-Republican Party.

# 520.

He declined offers to serve as Secretary of State and Chief Justice of the Supreme Court, preferring to focus on his law practice and private life.

# 521.

Patrick Henry was an avid supporter of agrarianism and believed in the importance of agriculture as the foundation of a prosperous society.

# 522.

He owned several plantations and was a successful tobacco farmer, accumulating wealth through his agricultural ventures.

# 523.

Henry was married twice. His first wife, Sarah Shelton, died in 1775, and he later remarried Dorothea Dandridge in 1777.

# 524.

He had a total of 17 children, with 11 from his first marriage and 6 from his second.

# 525.

Despite his political career, Henry preferred a more private life and spent much of his time on his plantation, Red Hill, in Charlotte County, Virginia.

# 526.

Henry's views on slavery evolved over time, and he became increasingly critical of the institution, expressing concerns about its moral implications and the impact on individual freedom.

# 527.

He advocated for gradual emancipation and the abolition of the international slave trade.

# 528.

Henry was a strong advocate for education and believed in the importance of an educated citizenry for the success of a democratic society.

# 529.

He helped establish Hampden-Sydney College in Virginia, serving as a trustee and providing financial support for the institution.

# 530.

Henry's speeches and writings continue to be studied and revered as powerful examples of persuasive rhetoric and political oratory.

## 531.

He was known for his captivating speaking style, using vivid imagery, emotional appeals, and rhetorical devices to engage his audience and convey his message.

## 532.

Henry was a respected lawyer, known for his skills in courtroom advocacy and his ability to present compelling arguments to juries.

## 533.

He frequently defended the rights of individuals and championed the principle of "innocent until proven guilty" in legal proceedings.

## 534.

Henry's legacy extends beyond his political contributions. He is also remembered for his efforts to promote economic development in Virginia, supporting initiatives such as canal construction and the improvement of transportation infrastructure.

## 535.

He was a strong advocate for states' rights and the preservation of individual liberties, often challenging the power and authority of the federal government.

## 536.

Henry's commitment to freedom and his passionate defense of liberty inspired many future leaders and became an enduring symbol of American revolutionary spirit.

## 537.

In addition to his political career, Henry was a successful planter and businessman, accumulating considerable wealth through his agricultural pursuits and land speculation.

# 538.

He was known for his strong work ethic and determination, often dedicating long hours to his legal practice and public service.

# 539.

Henry's speeches and writings were widely circulated and played a significant role in shaping public opinion during the Revolutionary era.

# 540.

He was instrumental in rallying support for the Virginia militia and played a crucial role in organizing and training troops for the defense of the state.

# 541.

Henry's advocacy for individual rights and limited government influenced the drafting of the United States Bill of Rights and the inclusion of key protections for citizens.

# 542.

He was an influential figure in Virginia politics, helping to establish the Democratic-Republican Party and shaping the state's political landscape for years to come.

# 543.

Henry's commitment to liberty and his passionate defense of American independence earned him the admiration of his contemporaries and subsequent generations.

# 544.

He was known for his humility and simplicity, often eschewing the trappings of power and maintaining a modest lifestyle.

# 545.

Henry's impact on American history is significant, as his speeches and writings continue to inspire and resonate with those advocating for freedom and individual rights.

## 546.

He played a key role in the development of a strong central government in Virginia, helping to shape the state's constitution and institutions.

## 547.

Henry's political philosophy emphasized the importance of limited government, individual liberty, and the right of the people to hold their elected representatives accountable.

## 548.

He was a dedicated patriot, risking his personal and professional life in the pursuit of American independence and the establishment of a free nation.

## 549.

Henry's commitment to the principles of the American Revolution extended beyond his own interests, as he actively supported and mentored younger revolutionary leaders.

## 550.

His legacy as a founding father and influential statesman is commemorated through various monuments, including the Patrick Henry National Memorial in Virginia, which honors his contributions to American history.

## 551.

The Kake Cannery is located in the small coastal town of Kake, Alaska, on the western shore of Kupreanof Island.

## 552.

It was established in 1912 by the Libby, McNeil & Libby Company, a prominent American canned food company.

## 553.

The cannery played a significant role in the commercial fishing industry of Southeast Alaska during the early 20th century.

## 554.

Kake Cannery was primarily involved in the processing of salmon, which was abundant in the nearby waters.

## 555.

The cannery provided employment opportunities for the local population, including Native Alaskans from the Tlingit community.

## 556.

At its peak, the cannery employed hundreds of workers during the fishing season.

## 557.

It had a self-contained operation with facilities for canning, processing, and shipping the canned fish.

## 558.

The cannery featured a large fish processing plant, warehouses for storing canned goods, and employee housing facilities.

## 559.

Kake Cannery had its own power plant to generate electricity for the operation.

## 560.

The cannery's location allowed for easy access to the fishing grounds, as the nearby waters were rich in salmon.

# 561.

Kake Cannery employed advanced canning technology and machinery, ensuring efficient and high-quality processing of fish.

# 562.

The canned salmon produced at the cannery was shipped to markets across the United States.

# 563.

Kake Cannery played a vital role in the local economy, contributing to the growth and development of the town of Kake.

# 564.

It provided a steady source of income for many families in the region, helping to support the local community.

# 565.

The cannery's operation was seasonal, with the fishing season typically lasting from spring to late summer.

# 566.

During the fishing season, the cannery operated around the clock, processing and canning salmon.

# 567.

The cannery employed a diverse workforce, including fishermen, cannery workers, packers, and administrative staff.

# 568.

Workers at the cannery often lived in company-provided housing, which fostered a close-knit community atmosphere.

# 569.

Kake Cannery was an important social hub, with workers engaging in recreational activities and community events during their downtime.

## 570.

The cannery also had a company store where workers could purchase goods and supplies.

## 571.

Kake Cannery faced challenges such as fluctuating fish populations, changing market conditions, and the occasional downturn in the fishing industry.

## 572.

In the early 1930s, the cannery faced financial difficulties and was temporarily closed, but it resumed operations in later years.

## 573.

During World War II, the cannery was utilized for military purposes, as it was near the strategic airfield on Kupreanof Island.

## 574.

After the war, the cannery returned to its primary function of processing and canning salmon.

## 575.

The decline of the salmon population in the nearby waters eventually led to the closure of Kake Cannery in the late 1950s.

## 576.

The closure of the cannery had a significant impact on the local economy, as it resulted in the loss of jobs and decreased economic activity in Kake.

# 577.

Today, the Kake Cannery is a historic site, serving as a reminder of the region's rich fishing heritage.

# 578.

The cannery buildings still stand, albeit in a state of disrepair, and offer a glimpse into the industrial history of the area.

# 579.

Efforts have been made to preserve and restore parts of the cannery site, aiming to showcase its historical significance.

# 580.

Kake Cannery is recognized as a significant cultural site for the Tlingit people, who have a deep connection to the land and sea.

# 581.

The cannery's closure prompted many workers and their families to relocate to other communities in search of employment opportunities.

# 582.

Some former cannery workers went on to establish their own fishing operations or pursue different career paths.

# 583.

The legacy of Kake Cannery is remembered and celebrated through storytelling, oral traditions, and cultural events in the community.

# 584.

The cannery site serves as a place of remembrance for those who worked and lived there, evoking memories of the past.

# 585.

Archaeological surveys and research have been conducted at the cannery site to uncover its historical significance and inform preservation efforts.

## 586.

The Kake Tribal Corporation, in collaboration with community members and organizations, works towards the preservation and revitalization of the cannery site.

## 587.

The Kake Cannery site offers educational opportunities for visitors interested in learning about the history of the fishing industry in Alaska.

## 588.

It serves as a reminder of the challenges and successes experienced by the people who worked in the cannery.

## 589.

The cannery's story is intertwined with the broader history of the fishing industry in Alaska, highlighting the economic importance of the region.

## 590.

Kake Cannery is a symbol of resilience and adaptability, reflecting the determination of the workers and their ability to overcome challenges.

## 591.

The site provides a unique perspective on the industrialization of fishing and the impact it had on the local environment and communities.

## 592.

The cannery's operation relied on the sustainable management of fish stocks to ensure long-term viability.

# 593.

Kake Cannery contributed to the development of modern fishing practices, including advancements in processing and preservation techniques.

# 594.

The cannery's closure sparked conversations about the need for sustainable fishing practices and the conservation of natural resources.

# 595.

The former cannery site has the potential to be developed into a cultural center or museum, showcasing the history and heritage of the fishing industry.

# 596.

The stories and experiences of the workers at Kake Cannery provide insights into the social dynamics and working conditions of the time.

# 597.

The cannery's location on the picturesque Alaskan coast adds to its charm and makes it an attractive destination for history enthusiasts.

# 598.

Kake Cannery serves as a focal point for community engagement and efforts to preserve the cultural heritage of the region.

# 599.

The cannery's legacy continues to shape the identity of Kake as a fishing community, instilling a sense of pride in its residents.

# 600.

The preservation and recognition of Kake Cannery's historical significance contribute to the broader understanding and appreciation of Alaska's fishing heritage.

# 601.

The Kennecott Mines, also known as Kennecott Copper Mines, are located in Wrangell-St. Elias National Park and Preserve, Alaska.

# 602.

The mines were discovered in 1900 by prospectors Jack Smith and Clarence Warner, who recognized the rich copper deposits in the area.

# 603.

The name "Kennecott" is derived from the Kennicott Glacier, which flows nearby. The spelling of the mine's name differs from the glacier due to a clerical error.

# 604.

The copper ore deposits at Kennecott were some of the richest in the world, containing high concentrations of copper, as well as other valuable minerals such as gold and silver.

# 605.

The Kennecott Mines became one of the most productive copper mines in history, yielding over 4.6 million tons of ore during its operational years.

# 606.

To access the copper deposits, the mines required extensive infrastructure, including a 196-mile railroad from Cordova to the minesite.

## 607.

The construction of the Copper River and Northwestern Railway, which connected the mines to the coast, was a remarkable engineering feat of the time.

## 608.

The Kennecott Mines were operated by the Kennecott Copper Corporation, a subsidiary of the Guggenheim family's mining empire.

## 609.

The mining operation at Kennecott was not limited to underground mining. Open-pit mining methods were also employed to extract the copper ore.

## 610.

The iconic red mill building at Kennecott, known as the Concentration Mill, was built in 1911. It processed the raw copper ore into a concentrated form.

## 611.

The Concentration Mill was an architectural marvel, featuring an innovative design and state-of-the-art machinery for its time.

## 612.

The Kennecott Mines had a profound impact on the development of Alaska, attracting thousands of people to the remote region in search of employment and economic opportunities.

## 613.

The mining operation at Kennecott required a large workforce, which included miners, engineers, geologists, mechanics, and support staff.

## 614.

The population of Kennecott and its associated town, McCarthy, grew rapidly during the mining boom, reaching around 500 residents at its peak.

## 615.

The town of Kennecott had its own school, hospital, general store, and recreational facilities to cater to the needs of the mining community.

## 616.

The workers at Kennecott Mines faced numerous challenges, including harsh weather conditions, isolation, and the risks associated with mining operations.

## 617.

The copper mined at Kennecott played a crucial role in the electrification of America, as it was used to produce wiring for electrical systems.

## 618.

World War I increased the demand for copper, leading to a period of intense mining activity at Kennecott during the war years.

## 619.

The decline of copper prices in the 1930s, coupled with the depletion of easily accessible ore, led to the closure of the Kennecott Mines in 1938.

## 620.

After the closure, the Kennecott Mines remained abandoned for decades, becoming a ghost town in the wilderness.

## 621.

In the 1970s, the National Park Service acquired the Kennecott Mines and embarked on a project to preserve and restore the historic buildings.

## 622.

The Kennecott Mines, along with the town of McCarthy, were designated a National Historic Landmark in 1986.

## 623.

Today, the Kennecott Mines and McCarthy are popular tourist destinations, attracting visitors who want to explore the rich mining history and experience the wilderness of Alaska.

## 624.

Guided tours are available to explore the well-preserved buildings of Kennecott, including the Concentration Mill, bunkhouses, and other structures.

## 625.

The Kennecott Mines offer a glimpse into the industrial heritage of Alaska and the challenges faced by the early miners and pioneers.

## 626.

The surrounding area of Kennecott is renowned for its stunning natural beauty, with glaciers, mountains, and rivers providing a picturesque backdrop.

## 627.

The Kennecott Glacier, which originates near the mines, is one of the largest glaciers in North America.

## 628.

The Kennecott Mines are situated within the boundaries of Wrangell-St. Elias National Park and Preserve, the largest national park in the United States.

## 629.

The park is known for its diverse wildlife, including grizzly bears, wolves, moose, and mountain goats.

## 630.

Hiking trails in the vicinity of Kennecott provide opportunities for outdoor enthusiasts to explore the rugged Alaskan wilderness.

## 631.

The Kennecott Mines and the surrounding area have been featured in several documentaries, books, and films, showcasing their historical significance and natural beauty.

## 632.

The Kennecott Mines are a testament to human ingenuity and determination, as the miners overcame immense challenges to extract valuable resources from a remote and unforgiving landscape.

## 633.

The abandoned buildings of Kennecott offer a hauntingly beautiful scene, with rusty machinery and crumbling structures contrasting against the pristine wilderness.

## 634.

The Kennecott Mines have attracted artists, photographers, and writers, who have captured the unique atmosphere and history of the place.

## 635.

The presence of the Kennecott Mines has contributed to scientific research, as geologists and ecologists study the region's geological formations and ecosystems.

# 636.

The Kennecott Mines serve as a reminder of the impact of mining activities on the environment, sparking discussions about responsible resource extraction and conservation.

# 637.

The area around Kennecott is known for its mineral wealth, with numerous other mining sites and prospects scattered throughout the region.

# 638.

The Kennecott Mines have been a source of inspiration for environmentalists and conservationists, highlighting the need to balance economic development with environmental stewardship.

# 639.

The Kennecott Mines played a role in the development of Alaska's mining regulations and environmental policies, shaping the state's approach to resource extraction.

# 640.

The isolation of Kennecott during its operational years led to a self-sufficient community, where residents relied on their resourcefulness to meet their needs.

# 641.

The Kennecott Mines were connected to the outside world through the Copper River and Northwestern Railway, which transported supplies and ore to and from the mines.

# 642.

The Kennecott Mines were known for their excellent safety record, thanks to rigorous safety protocols and employee training.

## 643.

The legacy of the Kennecott Mines lives on through the stories and memories of former workers and their descendants, who share their experiences with visitors.

## 644.

The restoration efforts at Kennecott have focused on preserving the authenticity of the site, allowing visitors to step back in time and imagine life during the mining era.

## 645.

The Kennecott Mines are an important cultural and historical site for Alaska Natives, who have ancestral ties to the land and the resources it provided.

## 646.

The copper extracted from the Kennecott Mines played a significant role in the industrialization of the United States, contributing to the growth of cities and infrastructure.

## 647.

The Kennecott Mines symbolize the perseverance and determination of those who sought fortune and opportunity in the Alaskan wilderness.

## 648.

The abandonment of Kennecott after its closure created a unique landscape, where nature reclaimed the structures, blending human history with the natural environment.

## 649.

The Kennecott Mines have been a subject of study for historians, archaeologists, and geologists, shedding light on the social, economic, and geological aspects of the region's history.

# 650.

The preservation and interpretation of the Kennecott Mines ensure that future generations can appreciate and learn from this significant chapter in Alaska's past.

# 651.

Africanized bees, also known as killer bees, are a hybrid of African honeybees and European honeybees.

# 652.

They were first introduced to Brazil in the 1950s with the aim of improving honey production.

# 653.

Africanized bees have since spread across the Americas, reaching as far north as the southern United States.

# 654.

They are known for their aggressive behavior and defensive nature, often attacking perceived threats in large numbers.

# 655.

Africanized bees have a faster attack response compared to European honeybees, making them more likely to sting.

# 656.

While individual Africanized bee stings are no more venomous than those of European honeybees, their aggressive behavior can result in more stings per attack.

# 657.

Africanized bees have been responsible for several human fatalities, although such incidents are relatively rare.

# 658.

The venom of Africanized bees is similar to that of European honeybees and can cause allergic reactions in susceptible individuals.

# 659.

Africanized bees are highly adaptable and can thrive in a variety of environments, from forests to urban areas.

# 660.

They are excellent foragers, with a preference for tropical and subtropical plants.

# 661.

Africanized bees are more likely to swarm than European honeybees, forming large groups that can be intimidating to humans.

# 662.

Swarming is the natural reproductive behavior of bees, where a queen and a portion of the colony leave the hive to establish a new one.

# 663.

Africanized bee swarms can migrate over long distances, often following the same routes year after year.

# 664.

Africanized bees are known for their resilience and ability to survive in challenging conditions, including droughts and harsh climates.

# 665.

The spread of Africanized bees has had significant impacts on the beekeeping industry, as commercial beekeepers have had to adapt their practices to manage these more aggressive colonies.

## 666.

Africanized bees are highly efficient pollinators and play a crucial role in plant reproduction and ecosystem health.

## 667.

Due to their aggressive nature, Africanized bees have posed challenges for agriculture, as farmers and workers need to take precautions to avoid bee attacks.

## 668.

Africanized bees have been known to take over existing honeybee colonies, killing the resident queen and replacing her with an Africanized queen.

## 669.

They have shorter development cycles compared to European honeybees, which allows for faster colony growth and expansion.

## 670.

Africanized bees have a tendency to build their hives in unusual locations, such as cavities in trees, walls, or even underground.

## 671.

The process of Africanization occurs when Africanized drones mate with European honeybee queens, resulting in hybrid colonies with Africanized traits.

## 672.

Africanized bees have a higher swarming frequency than European honeybees, which can make hive management more challenging.

## 673.

They have a strong instinct to defend their hive, with workers
quickly mobilizing to protect the colony in response to disturbances.

## 674.

Africanized bees exhibit a behavior called "fanning," where workers
use their wings to circulate air and regulate the temperature within
the hive.

## 675.

Africanized bees are highly sensitive to environmental changes, such
as fluctuations in temperature, humidity, and barometric pressure.

## 676.

They have a specialized alarm pheromone that triggers an aggressive
response within the colony when released.

## 677.

Africanized bees have been observed to exhibit unique defensive
behaviors, such as pursuing threats for longer distances compared to
European honeybees.

## 678.

Africanized bees have a higher tendency to rob honey from other
colonies, potentially leading to conflicts and aggression between
neighboring hives.

## 679.

The Africanized honeybee genome has been extensively studied to
understand the genetic basis for their aggressive behavior and other
traits.

## 680.

Africanized bees are efficient at building comb and storing honey,
making them prolific honey producers.

# 681.

They have a greater inclination to fill available comb space with brood (larvae) rather than honey, which can impact honey production in managed colonies.

# 682.

Africanized bees are capable of interbreeding with European honeybees, resulting in hybrid populations that exhibit varying levels of aggression.

# 683.

The spread of Africanized bees has prompted research into developing beekeeping strategies that promote coexistence with these bees while minimizing risks to humans and animals.

# 684.

Africanized bees are excellent at adapting to different floral resources, which allows them to forage and thrive in a wide range of habitats.

# 685.

They have been observed to exhibit increased defensive behaviors in response to human breath and vibrations, making them more prone to aggressive responses during close encounters.

# 686.

Africanized bees are more likely to respond aggressively to disturbances near their hive, such as loud noises or sudden movements.

# 687.

They are skilled at orienting themselves to their surroundings and navigating back to the hive even when foraging long distances from the colony.

# 688.

Africanized bees play a crucial role in the pollination of wild plants and crops, contributing to the overall biodiversity and food production in their habitats.

# 689.

Due to their strong swarming tendency, Africanized bees may create satellite colonies near the parent hive, increasing their overall population density in an area.

# 690.

Africanized bees have been studied for their potential genetic adaptations to diseases and parasites, as their survival in various environments suggests a certain level of resistance.

# 691.

Africanized bees have been successfully integrated into managed honeybee populations through controlled breeding and selection, allowing for the production of hybrid colonies with desirable traits.

# 692.

Africanized bees exhibit specific defensive behaviors, such as head-butting intruders, biting, and stinging, to deter threats to the colony.

# 693.

They have a unique flight pattern characterized by rapid, zigzag movements, which helps them evade predators and navigate complex environments.

# 694.

Africanized bees have a high colony density, often exceeding that of European honeybees in a given area.

# 695.

They have been studied for their potential as bioindicators of environmental pollution, as changes in their behavior and health can indicate shifts in ecosystem conditions.

## 696.

Africanized bees have been used as models for studying social insects and understanding the mechanisms underlying collective decision-making within a colony.

## 697.

They exhibit a remarkable ability to communicate through complex chemical signals, allowing them to coordinate tasks and convey information within the hive.

## 698.

Africanized bees have been used in agricultural systems for their pollination services, particularly in regions where other pollinators are scarce.

## 699.

The presence of Africanized bees has prompted the development and implementation of safety protocols for emergency responders and individuals working in areas with known bee populations.

## 700.

Africanized bees continue to be a subject of research and study, as their behavior, genetics, and interactions with other pollinators provide valuable insights into the ecological dynamics of honeybees in diverse environments.

## 701.

Allen's swamp monkeys, also known as swamp monkeys or Allenopithecus nigroviridis, are a species of Old World monkey found in the wetlands and swampy forests of Central Africa.

# 702.

They are named after Thomas Allen, a British explorer who first collected specimens of this monkey in the 19th century.

# 703.

Allen's swamp monkeys are medium-sized primates, with males weighing around 6-10 kilograms and females weighing slightly less.

# 704.

They have a distinct appearance with a blackish-green or olive-green fur color, long limbs, and a long tail.

# 705.

The face of Allen's swamp monkeys is hairless and has a pinkish or flesh-colored skin, which sets them apart from many other monkey species.

# 706.

They have a robust and muscular build, well-suited for their arboreal lifestyle in the swampy forest environments.

# 707.

Allen's swamp monkeys are highly social animals, living in large groups known as troops that can consist of up to 60 individuals.

# 708.

Within the troop, there is a hierarchical social structure, with dominant males and females having priority access to resources and mating opportunities.

# 709.

They are primarily diurnal, being most active during the day and resting or sleeping at night in the trees.

# 710.

Allen's swamp monkeys are excellent climbers, using their strong limbs and prehensile tails to navigate through the treetops and access food sources.

# 711.

They are omnivorous, feeding on a varied diet that includes fruits, leaves, seeds, flowers, insects, and small vertebrates.

# 712.

Swamp monkeys have specialized cheek pouches that allow them to store and transport food items, making it easier for them to forage and consume food later.

# 713.

They are known to be highly vocal animals, communicating through a range of calls, hoots, screams, and barks to convey messages within the troop.

# 714.

Allen's swamp monkeys are monogamous, with pairs forming long-term bonds and sharing parental responsibilities.

# 715.

Mating typically occurs during the rainy season when food resources are abundant.

# 716.

Female swamp monkeys have a gestation period of around six months, after which a single offspring is born.

# 717.

The newborn monkey is cared for by its mother and other members of the troop, receiving protection and support.

# 718.

Young swamp monkeys become independent at around 2 years of age but may stay within the troop until they reach sexual maturity.

# 719.

They have a lifespan of approximately 20-25 years in the wild.

# 720.

Allen's swamp monkeys have well-developed senses, including good eyesight and acute hearing, which help them navigate their environment and detect potential threats.

# 721.

They have been observed using tools in the wild, such as using sticks to extract insects from tree crevices or using leaves as makeshift umbrellas.

# 722.

Swamp monkeys have a complex social structure, with various social interactions and behaviors playing important roles in maintaining group cohesion.

# 723.

They engage in grooming behaviors, where individuals pick through each other's fur to remove dirt, parasites, and build social bonds.

# 724.

Allen's swamp monkeys are preyed upon by various predators in their habitat, including large birds of prey, snakes, and mammals like leopards.

# 725.

They exhibit a range of facial expressions and body postures, which are used for communication and expressing various emotional states.

## 726.

Swamp monkeys have been observed engaging in play behaviors, which help them develop physical skills, social bonds, and relieve stress.

## 727.

They are capable swimmers and are known to enter water bodies to cool off or escape from predators.

## 728.

Allen's swamp monkeys have been studied for their cognitive abilities, including problem-solving skills, memory, and learning capabilities.

## 729.

They are susceptible to habitat loss and fragmentation due to deforestation and human activities, which pose a threat to their populations.

## 730.

Conservation efforts are being undertaken to protect Allen's swamp monkeys, including the establishment of protected areas and education programs.

## 731.

They are considered a vulnerable species according to the International Union for Conservation of Nature (IUCN) Red List due to habitat loss and hunting.

## 732.

Swamp monkeys play an important ecological role as seed dispersers, helping to maintain forest diversity by spreading seeds through their feces.

## 733.

They have a unique odor that is used for individual recognition within the troop.

## 734.

Allen's swamp monkeys have been successfully kept and bred in captivity, contributing to the conservation and research efforts of this species.

## 735.

They are susceptible to various diseases and parasites, including malaria and ticks, which can impact their health and survival.

## 736.

Allen's swamp monkeys have been observed engaging in territorial behaviors, defending their home range from neighboring troops.

## 737.

They have a specialized digestive system that allows them to efficiently process a high-fiber diet.

## 738.

Swamp monkeys are known to display affiliative behaviors, such as hugging, kissing, and intertwining tails, to strengthen social bonds within the troop.

## 739.

They have well-developed spatial memory, allowing them to remember and navigate through their complex forest environment.

## 740.

Allen's swamp monkeys are known to exhibit curiosity and exploratory behaviors, investigating new objects or situations within their environment.

## 741.

They are highly adaptable animals, able to survive in a range of habitats, including primary and secondary forests, as well as swampy areas.

## 742.

Swamp monkeys have been studied for their vocalizations and communication systems, providing insights into primate communication evolution.

## 743.

They are susceptible to climate change impacts, including alterations in rainfall patterns and habitat degradation, which can affect their food availability.

## 744.

Allen's swamp monkeys are known to use different types of calls to warn the troop of potential threats, such as the presence of predators or intruders.

## 745.

They are considered a flagship species, representing the unique biodiversity of their habitat and promoting conservation efforts for the entire ecosystem.

## 746.

Swamp monkeys have a keen sense of balance and agility, allowing them to move gracefully through the treetops.

# 747.

They exhibit a high level of curiosity towards novel objects or situations, often approaching them cautiously to investigate.

# 748.

Allen's swamp monkeys are capable of recognizing themselves in mirrors, indicating a level of self-awareness.

# 749.

They have a remarkable ability to camouflage themselves within their surroundings, utilizing their coloration and body postures to blend in with the environment.

# 750.

The study of Allen's swamp monkeys provides valuable insights into primate behavior, ecology, and the importance of preserving their natural habitats.

# 751.

Joseph Hewes was an American merchant, politician, and signer of the United States Declaration of Independence.

# 752.

He was born on January 23, 1730, in Kingston, North Carolina.

# 753.

Hewes attended Princeton College (now Princeton University) and graduated in 1749.

# 754.

After completing his education, he entered the mercantile business, eventually becoming a successful merchant and shipper.

# 755.

Hewes served as a member of the North Carolina House of Commons from 1763 to 1775, representing the town of Edenton.

## 756.

He became actively involved in the resistance against British policies and supported the cause of American independence.

## 757.

Hewes was elected to the Continental Congress in 1774 and served as a delegate until 1777.

## 758.

He was one of the few Congressmen with extensive experience in trade, which made him valuable in dealing with economic and naval matters.

## 759.

Hewes served on various committees, including the Marine Committee and the Board of Admiralty, where he played a crucial role in building the American navy.

## 760.

He was appointed as the naval agent for North Carolina, responsible for purchasing and equipping ships for the Continental Navy.

## 761.

Hewes played a pivotal role in securing supplies and aid for the American Revolutionary forces, using his extensive connections in the shipping industry.

## 762.

He personally financed the outfitting of several privateers, which were instrumental in disrupting British supply lines during the war.

# 763.

Hewes was known for his frugality and simplicity, often wearing plain clothing and leading a modest lifestyle.

# 764.

He was deeply committed to the principles of republicanism and believed in the power of individual liberty and self-government.

# 765.

Hewes was instrumental in convincing the North Carolina legislature to support the ratification of the United States Constitution.

# 766.

He was elected as the first Secretary of the Navy under the new federal government but declined the position due to health issues.

# 767.

Hewes served as a trustee of the University of North Carolina at Chapel Hill and made significant donations to the institution.

# 768.

He was a strong advocate for the abolition of the slave trade and supported measures to restrict or eliminate it.

# 769.

Hewes never married and had no children. He dedicated his life to public service and the cause of American independence.

# 770.

He was known for his integrity, honesty, and unwavering commitment to the ideals of liberty and freedom.

# 771.

Hewes had a close friendship with fellow North Carolina delegate William Hooper and often collaborated with him on political matters.

## 772.

He was a devout Quaker and upheld Quaker principles of peace, nonviolence, and equality.

## 773.

Despite his Quaker background, Hewes actively supported the military efforts of the Revolutionary War, recognizing the necessity of armed resistance.

## 774.

Hewes was deeply respected by his colleagues and was often sought after for his advice and expertise.

## 775.

He was known for his exceptional organizational and managerial skills, which were invaluable during the war effort.

## 776.

Hewes was an advocate for fair trade policies and supported efforts to strengthen American manufacturing and industry.

## 777.

He played a key role in the development of the North Carolina shipping industry, helping to establish ports and trade routes.

## 778.

Hewes was a proponent of religious freedom and believed in the separation of church and state.

## 779.

He served as a member of the North Carolina Council of Safety, responsible for organizing and coordinating military efforts in the state.

## 780.

Hewes played a crucial role in the planning and execution of the Halifax Resolves, which called for independence from Great Britain and served as a precursor to the Declaration of Independence.

## 781.

He was elected as the first president of the North Carolina Provincial Congress, which governed the state during the early years of the Revolution.

## 782.

Hewes was known for his eloquent speeches and persuasive arguments, which helped rally support for the cause of independence.

## 783.

He was actively involved in trade negotiations with foreign nations, seeking alliances and securing supplies for the American war effort.

## 784.

Hewes faced significant financial challenges during the war, as his business suffered due to the disruptions caused by the conflict.

## 785.

Despite these challenges, he continued to contribute his own funds to support the revolutionary cause.

## 786.

Hewes was a strong advocate for the establishment of a strong central government and supported the powers granted to Congress under the Articles of Confederation.

# 787.

He served as a member of the North Carolina State Senate from 1783 to 1786.

# 788.

Hewes retired from public life in 1786 and devoted his time to his business interests and personal affairs.

# 789.

He passed away on November 10, 1779, at the age of 49 in Philadelphia, Pennsylvania.

# 790.

Hewes' contributions to the American Revolution and the establishment of the United States are commemorated by various monuments and memorials, including his tombstone at Christ Church Burial Ground in Philadelphia.

# 791.

His name is inscribed on the signer's plaque of the United States Declaration of Independence in the National Archives in Washington, D.C.

# 792.

The town of Edenton, North Carolina, has a historic district named after Hewes in recognition of his significant contributions to the town and the state.

# 793.

Several schools, streets, and buildings across the United States have been named in honor of Joseph Hewes.

# 794.

His life and legacy have been the subject of numerous historical studies and biographies, highlighting his role in the early years of American independence.

## 795.

The Joseph Hewes Award, presented by the North Carolina Maritime History Council, recognizes individuals or organizations that have made significant contributions to the maritime heritage of the state.

## 796.

Hewes' commitment to public service and his unwavering dedication to the principles of liberty and freedom continue to inspire generations of Americans.

## 797.

His contributions to the establishment of the United States Navy and his efforts to secure supplies and aid for the Revolutionary War were vital to the success of the American cause.

## 798.

Hewes' legacy as a statesman and patriot is celebrated for his pivotal role in shaping the early years of American independence.

## 799.

He is remembered as a true champion of American values, advocating for individual rights, representative government, and the pursuit of happiness.

## 800.

Joseph Hewes' life and work exemplify the sacrifices and contributions made by the founding generation of the United States, leaving a lasting impact on the nation's history and its ongoing pursuit of liberty and justice for all.

# 801.

Thomas Heyward Jr. was an American lawyer, planter, and signer of the United States Declaration of Independence.

# 802.

He was born on July 28, 1746, in St. Luke's Parish, South Carolina.

# 803.

Heyward attended the College of New Jersey (now Princeton University) and graduated in 1766.

# 804.

He studied law and was admitted to the South Carolina bar in 1773, establishing a successful legal practice.

# 805.

Heyward became involved in the American Revolutionary movement and actively supported the cause of independence.

# 806.

He served as a delegate to the First and Second Provincial Congresses of South Carolina, where he advocated for the rights of the colonists.

# 807.

Heyward was elected to the Continental Congress in 1775 and served until 1778.

# 808.

He was one of the youngest signers of the Declaration of Independence, affixing his signature at the age of 30.

# 809.

Heyward played a crucial role in drafting South Carolina's first constitution in 1776.

# 810.

He served on various committees in the Continental Congress, including the Committee on Indian Affairs and the Board of War.

# 811.

Heyward was captured by the British during the siege of Charleston in 1780 and spent nearly a year as a prisoner of war.

# 812.

He was held on a British prison ship and later in St. Augustine, Florida, before being exchanged for a British prisoner in July 1781.

# 813.

Heyward returned to South Carolina and resumed his legal practice after his release.

# 814.

He served in the South Carolina House of Representatives from 1782 to 1784 and was a member of the state convention that ratified the United States Constitution in 1788.

# 815.

Heyward was appointed as a judge of the South Carolina Court of Common Pleas and General Sessions in 1790.

# 816.

He supported the creation of a national bank and other economic measures proposed by Alexander Hamilton.

# 817.

Heyward was known for his strong opposition to slavery and spoke out against the institution both during and after his time in Congress.

## 818.

He played a significant role in the development of the education system in South Carolina, advocating for public schools and the establishment of a state university.

## 819.

Heyward was a devout Christian and actively supported religious freedom, advocating for the separation of church and state.

## 820.

He was a member of the St. James' Goose Creek Episcopal Church in South Carolina.

## 821.

Heyward was a founding member of the Agricultural Society of South Carolina, promoting advancements in agriculture and land management.

## 822.

He was an avid horticulturist and maintained a large plantation, where he experimented with new farming techniques and crop varieties.

## 823.

Heyward married Elizabeth Savage in 1773, and they had at least six children together.

## 824.

After his retirement from public life, Heyward focused on managing his plantation and overseeing the education and upbringing of his children.

# 825.

He corresponded with fellow Founding Fathers, including Thomas Jefferson and John Adams, discussing political and philosophical matters.

# 826.

Heyward's home, known as the Heyward-Washington House, is now a historic site and museum in Charleston, South Carolina.

# 827.

He was an early advocate for the construction of roads and infrastructure improvements to facilitate trade and economic development.

# 828.

Heyward was known for his strong moral character and integrity, earning the respect and admiration of his peers.

# 829.

He was deeply committed to the principles of liberty and justice, actively working to uphold the ideals of the American Revolution.

# 830.

Heyward's legal training and expertise made him a valuable asset in drafting legislation and interpreting laws.

# 831.

He was known for his eloquent speeches and persuasive arguments, which helped shape public opinion and rally support for the cause of independence.

# 832.

Heyward was a staunch defender of states' rights and believed in a limited role for the federal government.

## 833.

He played a key role in the development of South Carolina's legal system and judicial processes.

## 834.

Heyward's contributions to the American Revolution and the founding of the United States are commemorated by various monuments and memorials.

## 835.

His name is inscribed on the signer's plaque of the United States Declaration of Independence in the National Archives in Washington, D.C.

## 836.

Several schools, streets, and buildings across the United States have been named in honor of Thomas Heyward Jr.

## 837.

Heyward's life and legacy have been the subject of numerous historical studies and biographies, highlighting his role in shaping the early years of American independence.

## 838.

The Heyward family has a long and distinguished history in South Carolina, with several generations contributing to the state's development and governance.

## 839.

Thomas Heyward Jr. died on March 6, 1809, at the age of 62, in Jasper County, South Carolina.

## 840.

His burial site is located at the Old House Plantation Cemetery in Ridgeland, South Carolina.

# 841.

Heyward's contributions to the American Revolution and his dedication to the principles of liberty and freedom continue to inspire generations of Americans.

# 842.

His legacy as a statesman and patriot is celebrated for his unwavering commitment to the cause of independence and his tireless efforts to secure the rights and liberties of the American people.

# 843.

Heyward's life serves as a reminder of the sacrifices made by the Founding Fathers and the enduring principles upon which the United States was built.

# 844.

He is remembered as a true champion of American values, advocating for individual rights, representative government, and the pursuit of happiness.

# 845.

The principles and ideals espoused by Thomas Heyward Jr. continue to shape the nation's identity and guide its path toward a more perfect union.

# 846.

Heyward's dedication to public service and his unwavering commitment to the principles of liberty and justice exemplify the best of American patriotism.

# 847.

His contributions to the establishment of the United States are recognized as instrumental in the nation's early years.

## 848.

Heyward's legacy stands as a testament to the enduring values of freedom, equality, and self-determination.

## 849.

His impact on the development of South Carolina and the nation as a whole cannot be overstated.

## 850.

Thomas Heyward Jr.'s life and work continue to inspire and educate, reminding us of the courage and sacrifice required to secure and defend the principles upon which the United States was founded.

## 851.

Kiska Island is located in the Rat Islands group of the Aleutian Islands in Alaska, USA.

## 852.

During World War II, Kiska Island was occupied by Japanese forces from June 1942 to August 1943.

## 853.

The Japanese occupation of Kiska Island was part of their strategy to establish a defensive perimeter in the North Pacific and disrupt Allied operations.

## 854.

The occupation of Kiska Island was known as the Battle of Kiska, although there was no actual combat during the Japanese occupation.

## 855.

The Japanese built extensive fortifications and infrastructure on the island, including barracks, gun emplacements, tunnels, and underground storage facilities.

# 856.

Kiska Island was heavily mined by the Japanese to deter Allied forces from attempting a landing.

# 857.

The island's occupation by the Japanese was a closely guarded secret, and the United States only discovered their presence after they had already left.

# 858.

The American response to the Japanese occupation of Kiska Island was the Aleutian Islands campaign, which aimed to reclaim the island and secure the Aleutians.

# 859.

The Battle of Kiska, fought between the United States and Japan, took place from August 15 to August 24, 1943.

# 860.

The Japanese forces had actually evacuated Kiska Island before the American assault, leaving the island uninhabited.

# 861.

The battle resulted in a significant loss of life for both sides, with the Americans suffering casualties from friendly fire and booby traps left by the retreating Japanese.

# 862.

Kiska Island was declared secure by the United States on August 24, 1943.

# 863.

The remnants of the Japanese occupation, including fortifications and artifacts, can still be found on Kiska Island today.

# 864.

Kiska Island is part of the Alaska Maritime National Wildlife Refuge and is known for its rugged terrain, volcanic landscapes, and diverse wildlife.

# 865.

The island's harsh climate and isolation make it a challenging place to live, with only a few research stations and temporary military outposts.

# 866.

Kiska Island has a rich archaeological history, with evidence of human occupation dating back thousands of years.

# 867.

The island is home to a variety of bird species, including puffins, auklets, and eagles.

# 868.

Kiska Island is part of the Pacific Ring of Fire and has several volcanic peaks, including Mount Recheshnoi and Mount Kagamil.

# 869.

The island's volcanic activity has shaped its landscape, creating rugged cliffs, lava fields, and thermal hot springs.

# 870.

Kiska Island is known for its abundant marine life, including seals, sea lions, and whales.

# 871.

The island's vegetation consists of tundra, grasses, and mosses adapted to the harsh Arctic climate.

# 872.

The Japanese occupation of Kiska Island left a lasting impact on the local Aleut population, who were forcibly relocated by the United States government during the war.

# 873.

The Battle of Kiska is often overshadowed by other major World War II events but is an important part of the Pacific theater's history.

# 874.

The abandoned Japanese fortifications on Kiska Island serve as a reminder of the sacrifices made during the war and the enduring impact of conflict on the environment.

# 875.

The Japanese Occupation Site on Kiska Island is a designated archaeological site, protected for its historical and cultural significance.

# 876.

The island's remote location and challenging weather conditions make it a popular destination for adventurers and outdoor enthusiasts.

# 877.

Kiska Island is accessible by boat or helicopter, and visitors must obtain permits to visit the Japanese Occupation Site.

# 878.

The island's landscape and natural beauty make it a unique and picturesque destination for photographers and nature lovers.

## 879.

Kiska Island has been featured in various documentaries, books, and films that recount the events of the Japanese occupation and the subsequent battle.

## 880.

The Japanese Occupation Site on Kiska Island serves as a memorial to the soldiers and civilians who were involved in the conflict.

## 881.

The site includes interpretive panels and exhibits that provide information about the events that took place on the island.

## 882.

Kiska Island is known for its challenging hiking trails and opportunities for wilderness exploration.

## 883.

The island's waters are popular for fishing, with salmon, halibut, and cod among the sought-after species.

## 884.

Kiska Island is part of the Alaska Maritime National Wildlife Refuge, which protects important habitats for seabirds, marine mammals, and other wildlife.

## 885.

The island's rugged coastline is dotted with sea caves, rock formations, and hidden coves, adding to its allure for adventurers.

## 886.

Kiska Island offers unique opportunities for studying volcanic activity and geological processes in a remote and pristine environment.

## 887.

The island's historical significance and natural beauty make it a site of interest for researchers, historians, and conservationists.

## 888.

Kiska Island is home to a wide range of flora and fauna that have adapted to the island's challenging conditions.

## 889.

The island's isolation and harsh climate make it an ideal location for studying the effects of climate change and its impact on Arctic ecosystems.

## 890.

The Japanese Occupation Site on Kiska Island serves as a reminder of the importance of preserving historical sites and educating future generations about the realities of war.

## 891.

Kiska Island's strategic location in the North Pacific has made it a subject of interest for military planners throughout history.

## 892.

The island has been the site of various military activities and operations, including Cold War surveillance efforts.

## 893.

Kiska Island's volcanic activity continues to shape the island's landscape, with occasional eruptions and seismic events.

# 894.

The island's waters are known for their rich biodiversity, supporting a variety of fish, invertebrates, and marine plants.

# 895.

Kiska Island is part of the Alaska Maritime National Wildlife Refuge's Visitor Use Management Area, which aims to balance public access with conservation goals.

# 896.

The island's bird cliffs are home to nesting seabirds, providing important breeding grounds for species such as puffins and kittiwakes.

# 897.

Kiska Island has a unique climate, characterized by cool summers, cold winters, and strong winds, making it a challenging environment for vegetation to thrive.

# 898.

The island's geological features, including volcanic peaks and lava flows, make it a fascinating site for geologists and earth scientists.

# 899.

Kiska Island is part of the traditional territory of the Aleut people, who have inhabited the region for thousands of years.

# 900.

The natural and cultural heritage of Kiska Island makes it a significant place of interest for those seeking to explore Alaska's remote and storied past.

# 901.

Ladd Field was an airfield and military base located near Fairbanks, Alaska.

## 902.

It was originally established in 1939 as a civilian airfield and was later expanded for military use during World War II.

## 903.

Ladd Field was named after Major Arthur K. Ladd, an Army pilot who died in a crash near the airfield in 1935.

## 904.

The airfield played a crucial role in the defense of Alaska during World War II, serving as a staging area for aircraft and troops.

## 905.

Ladd Field was the primary base for the 11th Air Force, which was responsible for the defense of Alaska's Aleutian Islands.

## 906.

The construction of the Alaska Highway in the early 1940s further increased the strategic importance of Ladd Field.

## 907.

The airfield had a 10,000-foot runway, making it capable of handling large aircraft.

## 908.

Ladd Field was equipped with radar and anti-aircraft defenses to protect against potential enemy attacks.

## 909.

The harsh Arctic climate posed significant challenges for operations at Ladd Field, with extremely cold temperatures and long winters.

## 910.

The airfield was located near the city of Fairbanks, providing a crucial link between military forces and civilian support services.

## 911.

Ladd Field served as a refueling and maintenance center for aircraft traveling to and from the Soviet Union during World War II.

## 912.

The airfield was a hub for transport aircraft, facilitating the movement of troops, supplies, and equipment to the frontlines.

## 913.

Ladd Field was expanded after World War II and became a key Cold War installation, serving as a base for strategic bombers and missile defense systems.

## 914.

The airfield was home to the 516th Strategic Missile Squadron, which operated the Nike Hercules missile system.

## 915.

Ladd Field was designated as Ladd Air Force Base in 1951 when the Air Force became a separate branch of the military.

## 916.

The base played a significant role in the defense of North America during the Cold War, with its strategic location near the Soviet Union.

## 917.

Ladd Air Force Base was deactivated in 1961, but portions of the facility were transferred to the Army and became Fort Wainwright.

# 918.

The airfield's runway, known as Ladd Army Airfield, continues to be used for military and civilian aviation purposes.

# 919.

Ladd Field was a vital training ground for Arctic and cold-weather operations, with soldiers and airmen undergoing specialized training in extreme conditions.

# 920.

The airfield's proximity to the Alaska Range provided opportunities for mountain and glacier training exercises.

# 921.

Ladd Field was an important center for scientific research, with scientists studying the effects of cold weather on aircraft and personnel.

# 922.

The airfield served as a staging point for scientific expeditions to the Arctic and supported research projects in fields such as meteorology and geology.

# 923.

Ladd Field hosted the Alaska Air Defense Command Headquarters, responsible for monitoring and protecting Alaska's airspace.

# 924.

The airfield was equipped with radar installations and early warning systems to detect and track potential aerial threats.

# 925.

Ladd Field played a crucial role in the development of Arctic aviation, with pilots and aircrews gaining valuable experience in operating in extreme weather conditions.

## 926.

The airfield's location in the interior of Alaska provided a strategic advantage, allowing for rapid response to potential threats.

## 927.

Ladd Field served as a hub for search and rescue operations, providing assistance to aircraft in distress or missing in remote areas of Alaska.

## 928.

The airfield's facilities included hangars, barracks, administrative buildings, and support infrastructure necessary for military operations.

## 929.

Ladd Field hosted various aircraft types, including bombers, fighters, cargo planes, and reconnaissance aircraft.

## 930.

The airfield's runway was capable of handling large cargo aircraft, enabling the transportation of heavy equipment and supplies.

## 931.

Ladd Field was a bustling military community, with personnel and their families residing on the base and participating in recreational and social activities.

## 932.

The base had amenities such as schools, a hospital, housing complexes, and recreational facilities to support the well-being of military personnel and their dependents.

# 933.

Ladd Field played a crucial role in the development of Alaska's aviation industry, with its infrastructure and support services laying the foundation for commercial air travel in the region.

# 934.

The airfield's historical significance as a military installation has been recognized, and remnants of its infrastructure can still be found in the area.

# 935.

Ladd Field's legacy is preserved through exhibits and displays at the nearby Alaska Land and Sea Military Museum, showcasing the history of military operations in the region.

# 936.

The airfield's role in protecting Alaska's airspace and supporting military operations helped maintain the country's security and defense during critical periods in history.

# 937.

Ladd Field's operations contributed to the growth and development of Fairbanks as a regional center in Alaska.

# 938.

The airfield's runway continues to be utilized for civilian purposes, supporting commercial flights and general aviation in the region.

# 939.

Ladd Field's strategic location and importance during World War II led to its recognition as a National Historic Landmark in 1985.

# 940.

The airfield's historical significance draws visitors and researchers interested in Alaska's military history and the role of aviation in the region.

## 941.

Ladd Field's contributions to the defense of Alaska and the nation are commemorated through memorials and plaques on the site.

## 942.

The airfield's operational history includes collaborations with other military installations and units, demonstrating the importance of interagency cooperation in national defense.

## 943.

Ladd Field's facilities and infrastructure underwent modernization and expansion over the years to meet the changing needs of military operations.

## 944.

The airfield's support services included logistics, transportation, communications, and medical facilities to ensure the well-being and readiness of military personnel.

## 945.

Ladd Field's training programs and exercises focused on enhancing Arctic survival skills, navigation in extreme conditions, and effective response to emergencies.

## 946.

The airfield's operations extended beyond military activities, with occasional humanitarian missions and support provided to local communities during emergencies and natural disasters.

## 947.

Ladd Field's legacy as a military base has left a lasting impact on the local community, with veterans and their families forming bonds and memories during their time stationed there.

## 948.

The airfield's location in interior Alaska offered unique opportunities for wildlife viewing, with the surrounding wilderness home to a diverse range of animals, including moose, caribou, and migratory birds.

## 949.

Ladd Field's historical significance is a testament to the sacrifices and dedication of the men and women who served there, ensuring the security and defense of Alaska and the nation.

## 950.

The airfield's story is a reminder of the importance of military readiness and preparedness in safeguarding national interests and protecting the freedoms we cherish.

## 951.

Alligators are large reptiles that belong to the Crocodylia order, which also includes crocodiles and caimans.

## 952.

They are native to the southeastern United States and can be found in freshwater habitats like swamps, marshes, and lakes.

## 953.

Alligators have a powerful bite force that can exert tremendous pressure, allowing them to crush the shells of turtles and other prey.

## 954.

They have a lifespan of up to 50 years or more in the wild.

# 955.

Alligators are known for their impressive size, with males reaching an average length of 10 to 15 feet, while females are generally smaller, ranging from 8 to 10 feet.

# 956.

They have a broad, rounded snout, whereas crocodiles have a more pointed snout.

# 957.

Alligators have a muscular body covered in tough, armored skin with bony plates called osteoderms.

# 958.

Their skin is typically dark in color, providing effective camouflage in their natural habitats.

# 959.

Alligators are excellent swimmers and can move quickly in the water using their strong tails.

# 960.

Despite their size, alligators are agile and can move swiftly on land as well, using a belly-crawl motion.

# 961.

They are opportunistic predators and will feed on a variety of prey, including fish, turtles, birds, mammals, and even other alligators.

# 962.

Alligators have a unique hunting technique called "sit-and-wait," where they patiently wait for prey to come near the water's edge before striking.

# 963.

They have special glands on their tongues that secrete a musky odor, which they use to attract mates during the breeding season.

# 964.

Alligators are known for their distinctive bellowing vocalizations, which can be heard during mating rituals and territorial displays.

# 965.

Mating season for alligators typically occurs in the spring, and females construct nests made of vegetation and mud where they lay their eggs.

# 966.

Female alligators are fiercely protective of their nests and will aggressively defend them against any potential threats.

# 967.

Alligator eggs hatch after an incubation period of about 65 days, and the sex of the hatchlings is determined by the temperature at which the eggs were incubated.

# 968.

The hatchlings are about 6 to 8 inches long and are vulnerable to predation, so they stay close to their mother for protection.

# 969.

Alligators have a unique ability to regulate their body temperature by basking in the sun or cooling off in the water.

# 970.

During colder months, they can enter a state of dormancy called brumation, where they remain in a burrow or underwater to conserve energy.

# 971.

Alligators have a complex communication system that involves vocalizations, body language, and even infrasound vibrations.

# 972.

They have well-developed senses, including acute hearing and eyesight, which enable them to detect prey and potential threats.

# 973.

Alligators have a highly efficient cardiovascular system that allows them to dive underwater for extended periods while conserving oxygen.

# 974.

They have a remarkable ability to regrow lost teeth throughout their lifetime. On average, an alligator can grow over 2,000 teeth in its lifetime.

# 975.

Alligators play a crucial role in their ecosystems as apex predators, helping to control populations of prey species and maintaining the balance of the food chain.

# 976.

Despite their intimidating appearance, alligators generally avoid humans and will only become aggressive if they feel threatened or provoked.

# 977.

Alligators have been around for millions of years and are often referred to as living fossils.

# 978.

They are considered a keystone species, meaning their presence has a significant impact on the structure and function of their ecosystems.

## 979.

Alligators are considered a conservation success story, as their populations have rebounded after being severely threatened due to habitat loss and overhunting.

## 980.

They are protected by laws and regulations to ensure their survival and maintain healthy populations.

## 981.

Alligator farming has become an important industry in some regions, providing a sustainable source of meat and leather products.

## 982.

Alligator skin is highly valued for its durability and is used in the production of luxury items such as handbags, belts, and shoes.

## 983.

Alligators are capable of remarkable displays of strength and agility, making them a popular attraction in zoos and wildlife parks.

## 984.

They have an incredible immune system that helps them resist infections and heal wounds quickly.

## 985.

Alligators have a special valve in their throat that allows them to breathe even with their mouths open underwater.

## 986.

Alligators have a unique method of cooling themselves down called "gular fluttering," where they vibrate their throat to release excess heat.

## 987.

Alligators have a powerful tail that helps them navigate through water and is used as a weapon for defense and hunting.

## 988.

They have been observed using tools in the wild, such as using sticks to lure birds within striking distance.

## 989.

Alligators have a specialized gland located on their lower jaw that secretes a mucus-like substance, which helps to prevent the growth of bacteria on their teeth.

## 990.

Alligators have an extraordinary ability to camouflage themselves in their environment, blending in with the vegetation and water.

## 991.

They have a unique method of thermoregulation called "countercurrent heat exchange," where warm blood from their core heats the cooler blood returning from their extremities, helping to maintain body temperature.

## 992.

Alligators are known to create "gator holes" in their habitats by digging into the ground, which provides a source of water during dry periods and serves as a refuge for other animals.

## 993.

They have a nictitating membrane, or a third eyelid, that helps protect their eyes while underwater.

## 994.

Alligators are territorial creatures and mark their territory with scent glands located on their throat and under their tail.

## 995.

Alligators have a remarkable ability to sense vibrations in the water, allowing them to detect movement and locate prey, even in dark or murky conditions.

## 996.

They are known to exhibit interesting social behaviors, including courtship rituals, territorial disputes, and group basking.

## 997.

Alligators have an efficient digestive system that allows them to extract nutrients from their prey efficiently.

## 998.

They have been the subject of extensive scientific research, providing valuable insights into various aspects of their biology, behavior, and ecological importance.

## 999.

Alligators are apex predators in their ecosystems, meaning they have no natural predators as adults. However, young alligators may fall prey to larger birds, fish, and mammals.

## 1000.

Alligators are a symbol of resilience and adaptability, with their survival for millions of years serving as a testament to their remarkable evolutionary success.